KW-278-421

Climbing Plants for Walls and Gardens

BOOKS BY

C. E. LUCAS PHILLIPS

The Small Garden
Roses for Small Gardens
The Rothschild Rhododendrons *(with P. N. Barber)*
Climbing Plants for Walls and Gardens

Cromwell's Captains
Cockleshell Heroes
Escape of the 'Amethyst'
The Greatest Raid of All
The Spanish Pimpernel
The Vision Splendid
Alamein
Springboard to Victory

C. E. LUCAS PHILLIPS

Climbing Plants for Walls and Gardens

HEINEMANN : LONDON

William Heinemann Ltd
LONDON MELBOURNE TORONTO
CAPE TOWN AUCKLAND

First published 1967

Printed in Great Britain by
Cox & Wyman Ltd,
London, Fakenham and Reading

CONTENTS

PHOTOGRAPHS

Photographs

DRAWINGS

Drawings

THANKS

I am grateful to the several hands that have very kindly helped me in the production of this book.

Mr F. P. Knight, Director of the Royal Horticultural Society's Garden at Wisley, has read the proofs and made valuable suggestions. Mr C. D. Brickell, B.Sc., the Society's botanist, has read the manuscript and proofs, kept me straight on tricky botanical detail and taken in good part my digs at his profession.

Mr Harry Smith has most obligingly provided nearly all the photographs and Mr E. C. M. Haes, B.Sc., has kindly done most of the drawings.

C.E.L.P.

CHAPTER 1

THE UNION OF HOUSE AND GARDEN

Hardiness – Town Gardens – Walls – Shade

THE ivy-mantled tower, the cottage embowered in a thicket of rambler roses, the Victorian villa swathed in Virginia creeper are all expressions of an impulse that lies secreted in the bosoms of most gardeners. What multisyllabic label the psychologists might give to this impulse I cannot imagine, but in simple terms it is an instinct to simulate the conquest of nature over the handiworks of man.

As the lianas writhe and creep over some ancient Indian city, as the buddleias and the willow-herb sprouted from the bombed ruins of London, as the toadflax creeps along the crannies of old walls, so does the gardener seek to throw floral shrouds over all manner of buildings or even deliberately erect some garden structure which he immediately proceeds to envelop with vegetation. All organic gardening – gardening of the style particularly pursued in Britain – springs fundamentally from an instinct to maintain the supremacy of nature, though it may well be the substitution of one order of nature for another. We see it most patently in the "crazy" paving and the dry wall which, when sprinkled with pretty floral toys, deliberately simulate the encroachment of nature in the footsteps of man's neglect.

No one, I hope, would throw a vegetative shroud over any ancient mansion or cottage of architectural distinction and even your modern architect might feel offended if you did so to his works today. Too many of our houses, however, have not been designed by architects or have been designed by daft, dull, or indifferent ones. Many a monstrosity has been made bearable to the eye by the bright mantle of Virginia creeper.

The Union of House and Garden

There is a much quoted axiom of design which declares that "the house should march out to meet the garden", which is a pretty way of saying that the house should be extended into the garden by thrusting out a terrace. I heartily approve of terraces, but I reverse the maxim to the intent that the garden should run up and embrace the house, thus making house and garden one home.

Wherever there is just excuse, the garden scheme should integrate the two by bringing as many plants as possible right up to the walls of the house, not always to climb up and smother them, but certainly to clasp their feet with shrubs or roses or whatever other floral enchantments most please the gardener and most suit the house. Here we see the important difference between a "climber" and a "wall shrub"; for wall shrubs may with complete propriety cluster at the feet of the most distinguished mansion and the most romantic cottage, the beauty of which would be obscured by the indiscriminate use of climbers.

Nor is it only the flowers and the foliage that should run up to embrace the house. The orchard may also with great profit clasp the walls with its arms. If only for the sake of thrift, one ought, before making any choice, to think of using whatever good walls or tall fences there may be for growing fruit.

On walls that face south or west (after one has assimilated the necessary skills) one can cultivate the choicest fruits that, in most parts of the country, cannot be safely attempted in the open garden. Of such are the luscious nectarine (surely the real fruit of the gods), the choicest pears, the finest of the greengages (which means the one and only 'Reine Claude'); and for other walls there are the hardy Morello cherry and cordon red currants and gooseberries, while in the wilder parts of the garden blackberries, loganberries and their kind can make good use of any undistinguished fences or boundaries.

However, fruit is not within the compass of this book and, with a little reluctance, we must put it on one side to consider the adornment of the house and garden with plants of pure pleasure.

Of course, the house is not the only object, and not necessarily the best one, to serve as an extension of the garden. There are sheds, garages and fences that need to be decently clothed; there are decadent or commonplace trees which may be swiftly scaled by high-seeking scramblers; there are hedges that call for some relief to their flowerless monotony; there are pergolas, screens, trellises, pillars and so on that we may deliberately erect for the express purpose of displaying the beauty of those plants that fling their arms wide and far; and there are summerhouses and other scented and secluded arbours in which we may sit at ease to weave the garments of repose.

For all these uses a wide choice is open to us among those plants that have a naturally ascending habit or that can be induced to adopt one by the hand of man. For, as we should note from the outset, not all "climbers" will climb naturally. Some are mere sprawlers or tumblers along the ground. Leave a winter jasmine, a solanum or a rambler rose to itself and it is helpless to stand erect. Others (which we shall meet among the wall shrubs) in nature grow as normal open-ground bushes but, when planted against a wall, assume an ascending habit, leaning closely to their host; of this nature are *Euonymus fortunei radicans*, the flowering quinces (which we really must stop calling "japonicas") and various cotoneasters, ceanothus and pyracanthas.

Hardiness

Yet others again are grown against walls or fences or are screened by hedges simply because they are not sufficiently hardy to be exposed to the full rigours of the winter in open ground. We shall meet a great many of these, particularly the wall shrubs of Chapter 8. Gardeners in the east and north and midlands may well grind their teeth with envy and vexation as they read through these lists, but it is of no service to them to hide the facts, nor is it of service to those who live in the warmer and wetter counties of the west or the warmer and drier counties of the south coast to exclude such plants, as is often done in gardening books.

These balmy, maritime regions I frequently apostrophize in this book as the "Gulf Stream counties" in order to avoid constant repetition. This means the greater part of the south-west, parts of Wales, the west coast of Scotland, chosen places on the opposite shores of Ireland and similar climates in other lands. In these localities the winters are as a rule relatively mild, the air is moist from contact with the sea and there are bountiful falls of rain most of the year.

An extension of the Gulf Stream counties stretches eastwards from Cornwall along the southern shores of England as far as, say,

Brighton and for a distance of possibly twenty miles inland. Here it is warm and there is some influence from the sea, but there is relatively little rain. The Isle of Wight and Bournemouth can grow plenty of Gulf Stream plants, Winchester and Sussex some, but London very few and only under the protective shield of a south-facing wall. Thus in Cornwall the myrtles will grow proudly and tree-like in the open, but in London they are only modest bushes seeking shelter beneath a wall.

The practising gardener, however, knows well that, however professed tutors may define such matters, hardiness is often relative and comparative. There are parts of Cornwall and of western Scotland where gardening is a constant battle with the elements (particularly the wind) and, on the other hand, there are in our inland counties plenty of outdoor ingle-nooks, shielded from the north and east and lying above the level of frost pockets, where the beholder may be surprised by the vision of some exotic creature that would be killed stone-dead twenty yards away.

Thus in the cold heart of the Weald of Kent the Passion-flower may be seen to bear fruit and the glossy desfontainea outbraves the winter's rages in Edinburgh and Northumberland. The mutisia opens its enamelled rays happily in Inverness. On a hillside facing south, with the frost draining away into the valley below, one may be lucky enough in several counties to string the rosy bells of the lapageria against a warm but shady wall, to swoon under the amorous scent of the mandevilla and to lighten the shadowy places with the little lanterns of the crinodendron.

Town Gardens

Town houses may have very small gardens, but they have expanses of wall that usually exceed the area of ground. Thus they are often very well suited to climbing plants, which are in nature fully accustomed to being shut in by tall and over-shadowing obstacles. Many shrubs, herbaceous and rock plants, overawed by the surrounding high walls, are often frightened to death as they cower within the enclosures of very small town gardens. But the whole atmosphere of the place can be transformed by draping the walls of house and garden with sheets of honeysuckle, clematis, wisteria, the orange trumpets of the campsis, the summer and winter jasmines, the climbing hydrangeas, the creamy

Clematis montana climbing over an old tree

Above: A rose arch in the author's garden

Below: A rose pergola crossing a path in the author's garden

panicles of pileostegia, the sweetly scented trachelospermum, the little crimson lamps of schizandra or the diversified foliage of the more decorative ivies.

Thus even in towns one may effect the union of house and garden. Where the garden walls are not high enough or where otherwise there might be difficulties of display, screens, arches and pergolas of trellis, lattice or rustic poles expand the opportunities at little cost.

And if, as so often in old town gardens, there is some wistful and neglected tree – some mutilated oak or lime or some sad old apple, "its high top bald with dry antiquity" – it can be given new life and purpose by throwing over it a ceremonial robe of the red-and-gold celastrus, the scented holboellia, the high-climbing wisteria, the evergreen periploca, not to speak of the more familiar glories of the honeysuckle and clematis, which revel in spreading their cloaks over trees. The Virginia creepers, likewise, are seen in their most regal splendour when they clamber giddily to the top of an old oak, setting the autumn sky on fire as their leaves turn crimson. And always and everywhere there is the infallible, the resilient and the magnanimous rose.

The very small town gardens that are nowadays largely paved and any houses with basements may still be embowered in climbers by planting them in large tubs (bored in the bottom for drainage and layered with plenty of crocks) and wherever there is a balcony a veil of jasmine or solanum may be hung down the face of the house.

All these are quite hardy and may be grown pretty well anywhere in our islands. The adventurous gardener will not stop there, however, but, within the bounds of common sense, will make the small provisions needed for those many wall shrubs which hover on the brink of hardiness and which we shall discuss in Chapter 8. In localities where the grip of winter is too fierce for even these attempts there is always the greenhouse where,

> Unconscious of a less propitious clime
> There bloom exotic beauties, warm and snug,
> While the winds whistle and the snows descend.

So William Cowper in a familiar passage. As for the man who gardens in the atmospheric luxury of the Gulf Stream counties, all that is in this book is at his command and he will, indeed, disdain to give protection to those shrubs which in less favoured climates must have the protection of a wall, fence or hedge.

Walls

The main virtues of a wall, whether the wall of a house or a large old boundary wall (if you are lucky enough to possess one) are that it retains warmth, restrains buffeting by the wind and reduces the risks of breakage by snow. These advantages allow us to grow some plants that, when grown otherwise, are on the danger line of hardiness, such as the passion flower, the ceanothus, the nectarine and a great many others that have their places later in this book.

For these a **south** wall is usually the choicest. Indeed, nearly all climbers, hardy or tender (with reservations that will be noted later) will do better on a wall facing south than on others. Happy the man who has a south wall in the warmer counties on which he can display the splendours of the primrose jasmine or *Clianthus puniceus* or sniff as he passes the aromatic breath of the lemon-scented verbena. However, a possible danger of a south wall for some plants may be a soil too dry and thirsty and it will normally be unsuitable for the Chilean shrubs discussed in the next section.

A **west** wall is almost as good as a south one, and for those plants that like warmth without too much direct sun it is to be preferred.

An **east** wall will accommodate most plants that are generally hardy in that part of the country where one lives, but they present a special hazard to some plants that flower very early in the year. The abeliophyllum is an example. The shrub will be hardy enough, but its flower buds may be ruptured by too fast a thaw in the morning after a night's frost.

A **north** wall has usually been thought to be one of the gardener's most vexing problems, but in fact it need not be so, provided there is ample *light* and the wall is not overhung by adjacent trees nor unduly shaded by other buildings, such as the house-next-door. Among the clingers, there are the climbing hydrangeas and the ivies that will reach to the top of a house and (provided that you have the skill and patience to train it properly) the Morello cherry can also cover a very large area.

At a lower level on the north wall, but still reaching the top of the first floor windows, red currants trained as fans, cordons or espaliers will produce exhibition fruit. The pyracanthas will here put up a splendid show, densely draping the wall in an evergreen arras. Camellias, the golden trumpets of winter jasmine and *Euonymus fortunei radicans* are all quite content; and, scrambling over any or all of these, or trained to the wall itself, the coloured stars of the clematis will lighten the shadowy places.

A **north-east** wall is grimmer than a due-north one. In general, it can be treated by the same methods; but I would exclude camellias anywhere outside the milder counties of the west and south-west coasts. In subsequent chapters, I offer suggestions for the various aspects of walls.

Fences and hedges have some of the properties of walls and, if appropriately sited, break the ferocity of a north or east wind, but they hold little warmth.

Shade

Closely associated with the properties and the choice of walls is the matter of shade. A great many plants need full or partial protection from the direct rays of the sun, especially at their feet. This is particularly true of climbers, nearly all of which in nature take root in the shade of forests, woods and coppices and crawl along the ground until they encounter a tree, which they immediately mount in order to reach the light. In our gardens we think at once of the north wall or the northerly exposures of shrublands as the obvious place for shade-lovers. And this is excellent if the plant is a tough one, but, in general, such plants are fully content and, indeed, often put on their bravest show if their upper limbs are in full sun, provided that their feet are shaded, cool and moist.

One naturally supposes that plants from tropical or sub-tropical latitudes demand the full heat of the sun. This is normally true, but there is a small group of particularly handsome climbers and shrubs, immigrants from Chile, to which, in ordinary circumstances, this apparently obvious situation is likely to mean death, though not from simple heat-stroke. For, perverse creatures as they are, they obviously like warmth but they also expect shade, a very moist but not waterlogged soil and a fairly humid atmosphere. It is indeed remarkable how magnificently these gay strangers can grow in Northern Ireland and the west of Scotland, and sometimes elsewhere, surviving hard frosts simply because they have been given the right soil and the right situation. So far as we are concerned, this group includes particularly:

the desfontainea
the crinodendron
the berberidopsis
the lapageria
the "flame nasturtium" (*Tropaeolum speciosum*)

– all plants most ardently to be desired. The asteranthera, not quite so choice, has similar needs.

For these, heavy clay soils, desiccated sandy ones and chalk are all unpropitious. What is required is a turfy loam, such as is obtained by rotting down some turves, with plenty of leaf-mould or peat incorporated, plus rotted manure beyond the root tips at the time of planting, with a heavy annual mulch of leaves or bracken. This soil should be amply rained upon or watered throughout spring and summer and for most of this group of plants the soil should be an acid one. The berberidopsis seems to be an exception in being satisfied with a rather light, but not dry, soil.

The desire of these Chileans for shade seems at odds with their natural need for warmth; but shade comes into the picture mainly as an extra protection against too much transpiration by the leaves and it is of less urgency where the soil and the air are comfortably moist. Where these conditions do not prevail there is a problem. You cannot put these climbers and shrubs on a south wall unless that wall happens to be in shade – a condition we don't often allow in this country. A west wall gets a pretty hot sun all the afternoon. East and north ones are too cold. As far as wall plantings are concerned, we are therefore left with a north-west wall if there is one.

These requirements of soil and situation can be supplied in a great many parts of the country, but a moist atmosphere cannot be made to order and this is where the west coast scores.

The Methods of this Book

A few words at this early stage on the general arrangement of the book may be helpful to the reader.

After two chapters on cultural matters, I devote one chapter each to the rose and to the clematis, these being the genera of the widest application of purpose and needing discussion at some length because of their manifold species and varieties. After that, the climbers that ascend by clinging or gripping and those that do so by twining are segregated into two separate chapters, because of their different uses and needs. Then follow chapters on non-climbing wall shrubs and on annual and greenhouse climbers.

In this arrangement I have been guided largely by the uses to which the gardener may wish to put his plants. Usage has also, to some extent, governed the methods (or non-methods, you may say) of naming plants. It is unorthodox and for this I expect to be reproved. But, in common with the majority of gardeners, I prefer "honeysuckle" to *Lonicera* and "Virginia creeper" to *Parthenocissus*. Thus in the alphabetical lists a plant will be found under its vernacular name if it has one that is current in common speech, such as "ivy" and "passion flower"; but not when it has a fancy and fabricated one seldom used outside magazine articles and the like or used in only one or two countries, such as "tea tree" (*Leptospermum* species) and "flame nasturtium" (*Tropaeolum speciosum*). Of course, there are borderline cases, as in Cape figwort and the kowhai of New Zealand, but in nearly all instances there are cross references in the entries.

Nor have I stuck to botanical exactitude in nomenclature. These things are made more and more difficult for the gardener (and the writer) who is not trained in systematic botany and I have simplified them in what I hope is an acceptable manner, leaving out, for example, the hybrid sign × and bearing in mind always that what the reader wants is to know what to order from the nursery, which itself has usually only a rough idea of the orthodox names of plants. I also omit the term "var." where it should strictly be used.

Here and there I have made a few digs at the sort of botanist who is always changing the familiar names of things and turning what used to be a simple matter into an occult science, in which a straightforward page of print becomes "plagued with an itching leprosy" of signs, symbols, italics and inverted commas. We might well bear in mind what the poet said – that "the true names of flowers are in heaven".

I am botanically correct, however, in not falling for the new, stilted vogue-word "cultivar", which means a variety of garden origin as distinct from a variety occurring in nature. *The International Code*, which governs these matters, is at pains to emphasise that "variety" is the "exact equivalent" of "cultivar", the use of which is entirely optional, and accordingly I usually employ the more familiar word instead of the pedantic one.

For the benefit of overseas readers, I ought also to remark that in this book I do not use the word "vine" in the American sense, as applying to all climbing plants, but in the sense of the "gadding o'ergrown vine" of Milton, the Roman vine, the vine of Bacchus – to wit, the various species, edible or inedible, of the genus *Vitis*.

With the hope of helping the reader in his choice of plants for various uses, I have in nearly all instances given an indication of the heights to which he may expect them to grow. Practising gardeners, however, will know well that this can often be no more than an approximation and occasionally not even that. So much depends on the climate, the soil, the exposure, the skill of the gardener and the quality of the stock he buys. In suggesting these sizes I have assumed what might be called "good average" conditions for all these factors.

CHAPTER 2

THE HABITS OF CLIMBERS

Methods of ascent – The Means of Support – Pergolas and other Woodworks – Problems – Natural habits

Not everyone provides at the start for the fact that most ascending plants need a host other than a mere blank wall. The nature of the host may be determined by the means (if any) with which the plant is equipped for climbing. In the wild those that are natural climbers simply clamber up and over other plants, as we may see the wild clematis, honeysuckle and ivy clambering in our own woods and hedgerows. They may do so by adhering, by twining, by hooking on with their thorns or simply by flopping about.

We must therefore, at the beginning of our study, segregate the plants according to these various methods, in order that we may apply them to their most appropriate uses and provide them with that particular method of support which will best display their excellence and simplify our own task in growing them. The groups are:

Clingers. These cling to their host with little aërial roots (or, in the better American term, "holdfasts") or with suction pads and need no help from man once they are planted in the right sort of place. A few are of restrained stature, but in the main they are of strapping physique, equipped to mask large expanses of wall or to crawl giddily to the tops of tall trees. They include the ivies, the Virginia creepers and some good plants not commonly grown, particularly the handsome, trumpet-flowered campsis.

Twiners, twisters and **scramblers.** There are a lot of these. Some, such as the clematis and the Passion-flower, attach themselves to their host by twining tendrils or leaf stems; others, prominently the wisteria and the honeysuckle, twist their stems corkscrew-wise round their host, and very often round their own limbs also, like the serpents that throttled Laocoön. All these need to be provided with some sort of artificial means of support in the shape of a trellis, wire mesh or arch, unless planted to ramble over a host-shrub as in nature.

Several of these twiners and twisters take a delight in crawling along the backs of others. This is a propensity that we can turn to our advantage, as when we plant a clematis to creep up a wisteria or a pyracantha, so providing two or more floral displays over the same area of wall or screen during the season by an adroit choice of the right varieties. Ben Jonson, in his *Vision of Delight*, reminds us of this natural propensity, manifested in our own woods and hedgerows, when he commands us to notice

> How the blue bindweed doth itself infold
> With honeysuckle, and both these intwine
> Themselves with bryony and jessamine.

The twiners also include a few annuals or plants that we treat as annuals, especially sweet peas, whose employment in the manner that nature intended is often forgotten and which look enchanting when climbing up other climbers, particularly roses when they have finished their turn of duty.

Roses, which climb after a fashion by means of their thorns, are in a special class.

Wall shrubs, of which we have already spoken. These do not climb, but hug the wall for its warmth.

Floppers. Among these are the mauve-flowered solanum, the winter jasmine and *Forsythia suspensa*, which have no climbing propensities and have to be tied up by hand to artificial supports if we want to bully them into an ascending habit. Several roses, including the more lax-limbed ramblers, are among the floppers and certain of the wild species in fact grow flat on the ground.

The clingers and the wall shrubs offer no problems in the provision of a support, but the twiners, twisters, scramblers and roses do, if it is intended to grow them on walls, fences, pergolas, screens or pillars, rather than clambering over bushes and hedges. It is useless to attempt to grow them unless the right kind of support is given them, which means that it must be of sympathetic and durable material and high and wide enough for the full spread of the plants, or nearly so. To bunch them up on a wall with a bit of string tied to a nail is to make a mockery and a misery of them. Indeed, the aim should be to avoid being obliged to do any tying at all and to leave the plant to itself, but this is not always possible even in the best regulated garden.

The Means of Support

There are several methods of providing artificial hosts on walls and fences.

Wire grids. A traditional method, and inconspicuous, is to erect a framework of fairly heavy-gauge wire, tightly strained through vine-eyes driven into the wall by means of Rawlplugs and projecting about 2 or 3 inches from it. The horizontal wires can be about 9 inches apart and a few vertical wires will also be useful.

This method, however, can be used only on brick, stone or concrete walls, not on tile-hung or stucco walls. Indeed, no type of climbing plant of vigorous habit, other than a wall shrub, can be grown on a tile-hung wall, for the young shoots have the deplorable habit of sneaking in underneath the tiles, to the detriment of the wall and of themselves.

Straining wires can also be fitted to wooden fences by using screw-eyes, but can be fixed only to the posts and the arris rails.

Lattice and **Trellis.** Another method is by panels of wooden lattice or trellis work. The collapsible panels sold by household stores are not very good and it is far better to make one's own from 1-inch square wood. Square or oblong designs or designs of variable spacing look far better than diamond-shaped ones. Make the panels on the ground in the workshop or garage and treat them with a horticulture grade of Cuprinol or Solignum. Fix them to the wall by means of special brackets so that they project a good 3 inches from the wall. The same type of panelling is excellent for building a long rose screen, for filling in the sides of arches and pergolas and for increasing the height of wooden fences. A suggested design is shown in Fig. 1.

Chain-link fencing. A third and very easy method (of which I was one of the first practitioners) is to use the new plastic-covered chain-link fencing wire. This is obtainable in rolls in various colours, of which I find the black the best, because it is almost invisible. The close mesh and the soft surface make this an excellent host for

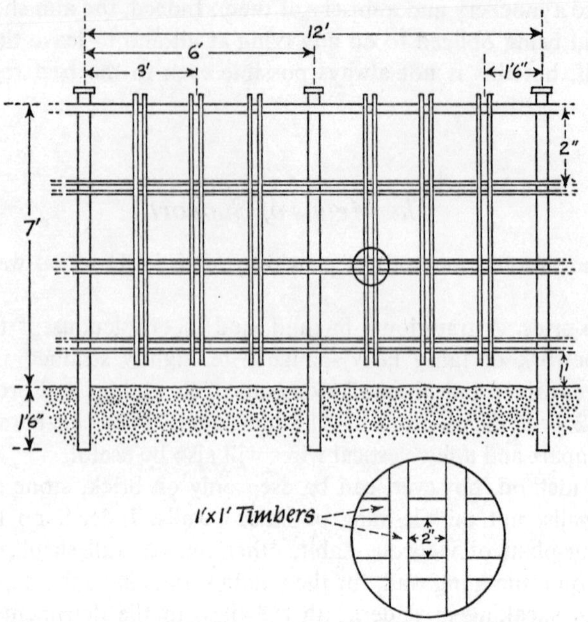

FIG. 1. A design for a lattice screen.

a great many styles of twining plants, particularly clematis and passion flower, as well as for roses, but it is not strong enough for the heavyweight climbers such as wisteria.

All you have to do is to cut the roll into appropriate lengths, drive a few nails into the wall or fence, hang up the wire on them and secure it at the bottom, sides and middle with one or two more nails. Your perfectionist who objects to putting nails into walls could use large cup-hooks instead, screwed into Rawlplugs.

There are now some light-weight substitutes for this fencing, no doubt good for small jobs.

Wall Nails. For small occasional jobs wall nails can be used, if with discretion. These are thick, square-headed nails with a flexible leaden flap attached to the head. The flap is intended to be twisted round the stems of the plant, but this is a reprehensible practice unless the shoots are slender and will always be so, as in some honeysuckles. It is preferable, though more tiresome, to use loops of leather or other material or good quality string.

These wall nails will not penetrate concrete but are useful for brick and mortar and on wood surfaces of any kind. They come in handy also for plants assigned to the duty of smothering outhouses and garages, where the more elaborate wooden or wire frameworks might not be justified. Other types of wall nail are also available.

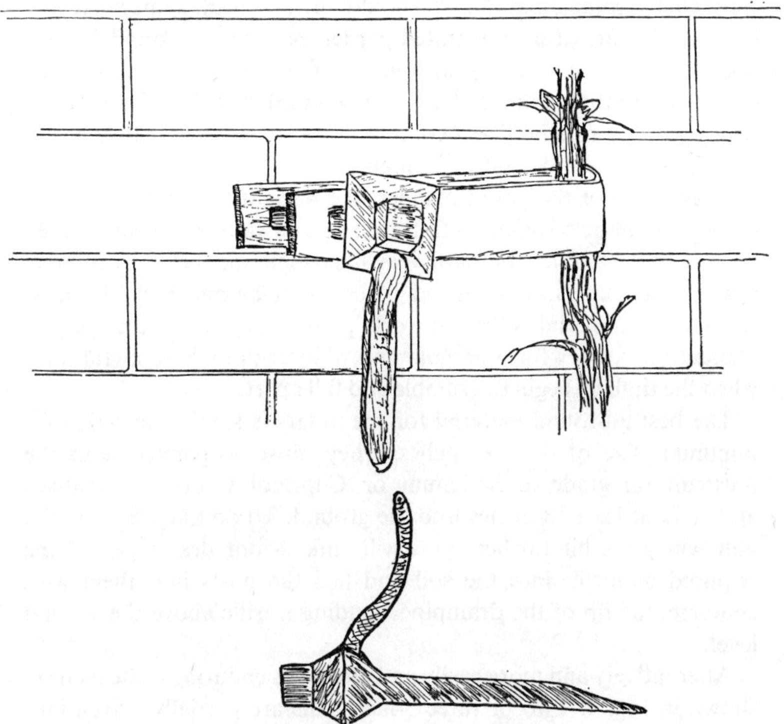

FIG. 2. *Below:* A wall nail of the type commonly available. *Above:* A loop of leather or strong cloth is taken round the clematis stem and the wall nail is driven through the loose ends into the wall.

Pergolas and Other Woodworks

The garden's third dimension may be provided naturally by trees or in a very different manner by the gardener's own handiworks. No tree, however, can supply the particular charms of a pergola and all forms of garden joinery have the advantage over trees in small gardens in that they have no spreading branches, which restrict the cultivation of a substantial area of soil. Pergolas, screens, arches and similar structures add elegance to the garden scene if well made and well sited. Badly sited, they are discordant. Badly made, they soon disintegrate into a picture of shabbiness and neglect.

A **pergola,** one may say, is a sort of floral cloisters or an openwork tunnel, beneath the leaf canopy of which one may perambulate in Marvellian contemplation. It should always lead somewhere, or form some part of an integrated garden pattern, not stand in purposeless isolation – a not uncommon fault in garden design. Its essentials are that it should have length and that it should be topped with overhead rafters, like a continuous series of arches. It ought to be at least 6 feet wide and 7 feet high.

In pergolas of the grand manner, the upright members will be of dressed stone or of brick, with transoms and rafters of heavy oaken beams. In a humbler, but still very handsome manner we can erect a structure that is all of wood of one sort or another. The least satisfactory material is "rustic work", which does not have the permanence necessary for a pergola and which will look an awful mess when the timbers begin to crumble and fall apart.

The best all-round material for the pillars is square-cut oak, of a minimum size of 4 × 4 inches. They must be painted with the horticultural grade of Solignum or Cuprinol wood preservatives and sunk at least 18 inches into the ground. To do the job properly, you will go a bit further; you will sink 2-foot drainpipes of the required diameter into the soil and bed the posts into them with concrete, the lip of the drainpipe standing a trifle above the ground level.

Alternatively and more easily and almost as enduring is the method shown in Fig. 4. Two or three 3-inch nails are partially driven into each face of the base of the post, projecting about 2 inches, and the post is dropped in to a hole 15 to 18 inches deep, which is then filled with concrete. The nails ensure a firm bond. The diameter of the hole must extend at least 1 inch beyond each nail, so that for a post 4 × 4 inches, the diameter would be a good 10 inches. The concrete filling must extend 2 or 3 inches above ground level (which is the point at which rot usually starts).

The distance between the pillars will depend on the strength of the timbers you choose for the transoms and rafters; normally 6 feet suits the case. All timbers except the pillars, if cost is an issue, can very well be of good quality softwood, provided they are thoroughly treated with preservative. The transoms may be either

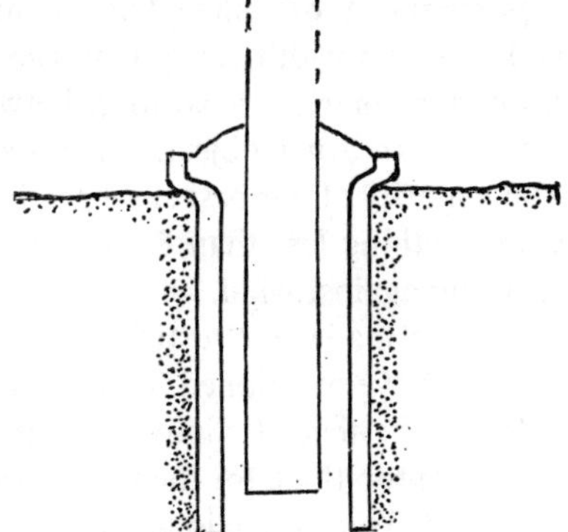

FIG. 3. Sectional sketch to show method of setting a post in concrete inside a drainpipe.

longitudinal, along the lines of the pillars, or else lateral, across the ambulatory. The rafters are laid on top of these and at right angles to them.

There remains the question of filling-in between the pillars. Very often there is none, with the result that the plants, whatever they may be, have to be bunched up to each upright before spreading out overhead. So it is much better to fill in every alternative pair of pillars with a panel of loose and open lattice work, such as that shown in Fig. 1, or else to stretch heavy-gauge wire between the pillars.

An alternative to the pergola is a system of posts linked together with catenary loops of rope or chain. This is well suited to the laxer roses and to a few other short climbers.

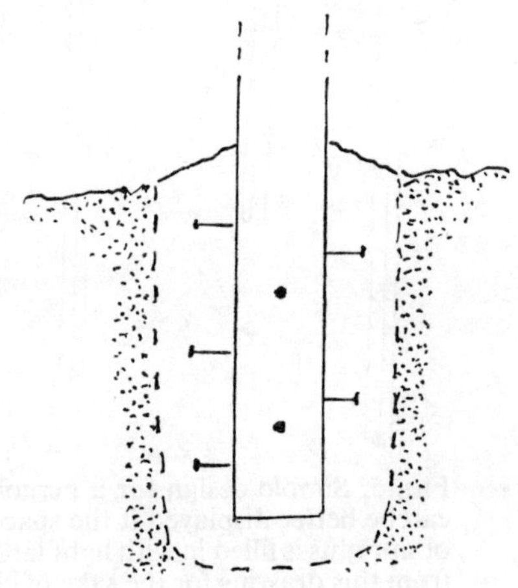

FIG. 4. A method without a drainpipe.

Screens can, of course, have many uses and are in effect tall, floral hedges of no width. They may run right down a boundary between properties, mark a separation between parts of the garden or mask some unhandsome object. Screens are generally made much too low. The majority of our best climbers, including roses, will not be satisfied with anything less than 8 feet, while anything more will need side-strutting against wind.

Screens made of "rustic" poles have the same drawback as that which I have mentioned for pergolas. Additionally, they are unsuitable for the tendril climbers, as the timbers used for the necessary filling are too thick for them to clasp. But stem-twiners and roses will not mind. Thus in the long term the sound thing is to build the screen of the same materials as the pergolas – oak posts sunk in concrete and connected by lattice work.

Arches, like pergolas, ought to be sited to serve some purpose and to fit into the general garden design, not just stuck anywhere over

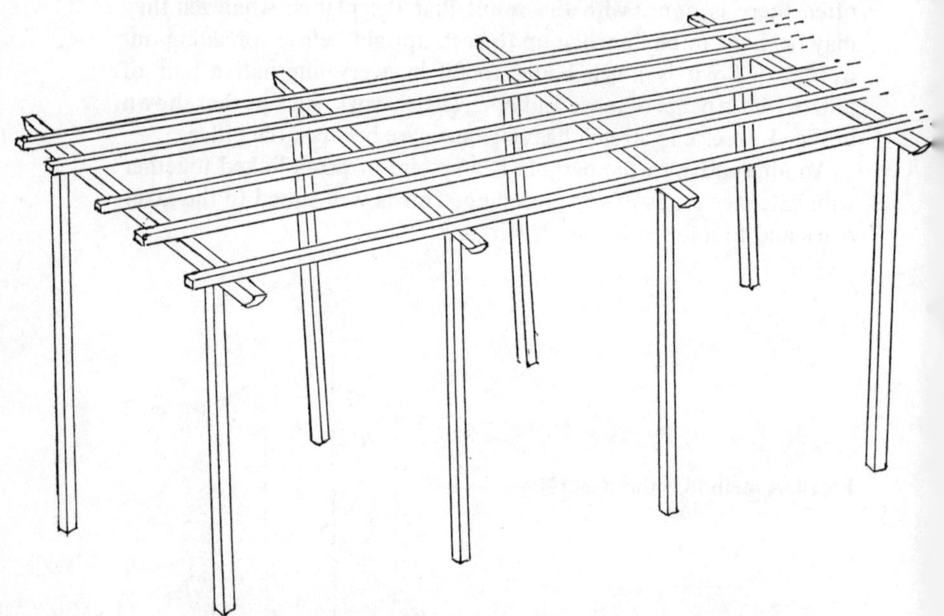

FIG. 5. Simple design for a pergola of squared timbers. Plants can be better displayed if the space between each alternate pair of uprights is filled in with light lattice work, as in Fig. 1 (omitted from this drawing for the sake of clarity), or with strained wires.

a path. They look most effective when they create a "frame" for some vista, as, for example, outside a door of the house or leading from one part of the garden to another. Broad arches, resembling the sections of a pergola, 4 feet wide or more, with four main pillars, are far better than narrow ones, allowing the plants to be well spread out.

Here, however, if the purse is not deep, larch poles, being easily replaceable, may well be used instead of oak, provided that they

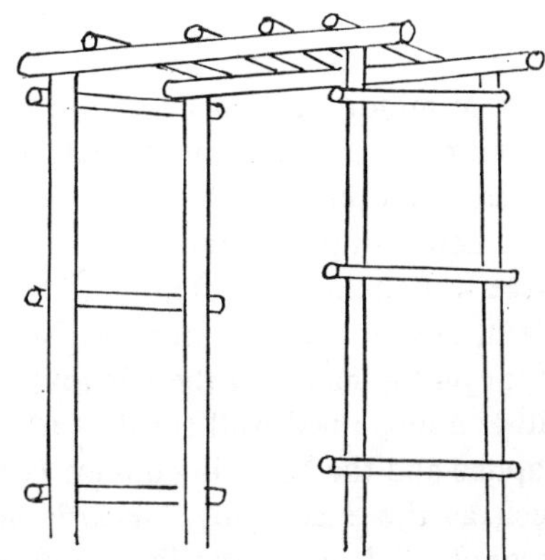

FIG. 6. A design for a "rustic" or other wooden arch.

are treated with wood preservative. But don't grow the tendril twiners on them, unless you grow a rose also as their host or unless you fill-in with the plastic covered chain-link fencing mentioned earlier or one of its substitutes.

Tripods are most effective dodges for giving accent notes in a garden composition. They may be of larch, oak or cedar, set in the ground in the manner of a wigwam, and 9 feet high, with the legs 3 feet apart. The rambler type of rose looks particularly well wound round the legs – more than one rose if you like – with a clematis or other twiner of modest height planted in the middle.

Arbours and **loggias.** These are the very things for climbing plants of nearly all sorts, especially the scented ones, reminding us of Hero's invitation to Beatrice to enter

the pleached bower,
Where honeysuckles, ripened by the sun,
Forbid the sun to enter.

Make them as high and wide as you like, of good materials, sited to enjoy some agreeable prospect and with special attention to the overhead timbers. The arbour will usually be out in the garden, whereas the loggia (which I hope you will pronounce approximately the same as "lodger") is a paved extension of the house. In these one may often grow plants in tubs or large pots, besides those in the soil outside.

Problems

Several minor problems that are not immediately self-evident tend to limit our use of climbing plants on the walls of houses, as compared with other walls.

A newly imposed one is the "picture window". These occupy a large wall space and often inhibit the use of any kind of ascending plant, but on a house not excessively fenestrated one can, of course, plant on the flanks of the window. Here one has two main choices: either a restrained wall shrub, such as abutilon, cotoneaster, hebe, daphne and the flowering quince (Chapter 8), or a slender climber, such as the enchanting *Clematis macropetala*, the many-tinctured *Actinidia kolomikta*, the Passion-flower and the lamp-lit *Schizandra rubrifolia*[1] (Chapter 7). The same sort of problem is presented by a house that has ordinary windows but a lot of them set close together. Here, however, one can guide the young shoots of many stronger climbers between and below the windows, after which they will usually need little attention.

A nasty problem often confronts the unwary householder when the unwelcome time comes to repaint the house. One has to be awfully circumspect in the choice of any climbers on walls that are faced with stucco, cement or painted timber. On such surfaces the only plants that may safely be chosen are certain wall shrubs, roses that have not grown to rampant dimensions and a few other climbers (such as wisteria) which it will be possible to pull away from the wall and wrap in sacking. All the clingers – ivies, Virginia creeper, campsis, the climbing hydrangea and so on – are definitely out. The painter will similarly be disgusted if he finds the wall covered with a wooden trellis of a kind that cannot be fairly easily unscrewed or jacked out.

To a less extent, and on any kind of building surface, we must

[1] The correct but rarely used appellation is *rubriflora.*

Rose 'Thelma' climbing on a holly in the author's garden, with a selected form of *Potentilla fruticosa* at foot

Trained pyracantha at Shoppenhanger Manor

Clematis tangutica

Clematis orientalis, the 'lemon peel' clematis

watch the drainpipes and the window frames when repainting. Drainpipes present another kind of problem also, apart from painting; the limbs of any plant that thickens and swells with age – such as wisteria, campsis, some roses and sometimes the clingers also – must be prevented from infiltrating between the wall and the pipe, or the pipe will before long be broken asunder.

Another practical problem one must be prepared to face is that of maintaining command over plants that get out of reach. Anything that needs to be tied in, pruned or otherwise tended will then mean mounting a ladder and imitating a seaman reefing the topsails. Anyone not prepared to be faced with this hazard had better stick to plants that grow no more than 6 or 7 feet or else confine himself to plants that are self-sufficient. The clingers can be allowed to run away by themselves until they begin to envelop windows and after some years reach the roof. On reaching the eaves all should be cut back by a foot, or damage will be done to the gutters.

Nature's Hosts

Having said all this about artificial hosts such as walls, fences, pergolas and so on, I must remind the reader that certain plants not only look most beautiful but also give the gardener the least trouble when provided with a natural one. This means a shrub, tree or hedge. For this kind of rôle the clematis is the actor *par excellence* and in the chapter on that delectable flower we shall consider its uses further.

Trees. We must not be led into supposing that to set a climbing plant to mount into the branches of a tree is a matter to be entered into in any haphazard fashion. There are several points to be weighed up. On the one hand we must not spoil a good tree and on the other hand we must give the climber a fair chance. Host and guest must be in harmony. It would be foolish to plant a climber beneath a large tree in full health and densely swathed with foliage, such as a beech, willow, chestnut or syncamore, or any tree with delicate foliage requiring no other adornment.

There are a few climbers that, given the right conditions, are capable of mounting to the tops of quite large trees; of such are the ivy, the Virginia creeper, the climbing hydrangea (*H. petiolaris*) and the noble vine *Vitis coignetiae*, superlative in autumn with its swags of huge, ensanguined leaves. But such associations are usually best confined to decadent old trees, which may in this manner continue a life of usefulness for a while.

For smaller trees, up to 30 feet or so and whether decadent or not, we have a wide choice of less rampant climbers, beautiful in flower or foliage; among them are several delightful roses, clematis, honeysuckle (with reservations), the potato-flowered solanum, the akebia with the violet sausages that you hope it will produce, the brilliant-seeded celastrus and lesser-known plants that will be encountered later on. Here again we should avoid requiring any small tree of special foliage beauty or any one of heavy and umbrageous leafage to act as host. For these less rampant climbers, appropriate host-trees are laburnums, crab apples, the columnar Japanese cherry 'Amanagowa', rowans, the taller dogwoods, hawthorns and eucryphias.

All these are desirable small trees in their own right, but are not spoilt by the choice of the right kinds of climbers. With even less hesitation, we may give new usefulness and splendour to an old apple or pear that is past its best. For trees midway between the small and the large, the wisteria and *Clematis montana*, the "virgin's bower", are the most dramatic of actors.

In addition to a wise choice of mates, other considerations confront us in the tree-climbing art.

The reason why plants climb, it may be said, is because they are eager to escape from the forest shade in which they were born and rush up into the light, where they will meet their friends the bees and where their leaves may become charged with the alchemy that invigorates their being. Accordingly, to encourage this propensity, we should as a rule not plant the natural climbers immediately in the light, but on the northerly quadrant of the tree. Planted in the sun, many will be disinclined to make the effort of climbing.

A point that exercises one a great deal is just where to plant the climber in relation to the tree, in order to be sure that the roots of the host will not strangle those of its guest. Contrary to general belief, the best position, as was pointed out by the late W. J. Bean when Curator of Kew Gardens, is as close as physically practicable to the trunk of the tree. The feeding roots of the tree are not here, but at or near their extremities.

Thus we have to dig out a plot close to the trunk and not less than 3 feet square or its equivalent and treat it in the manner prescribed in the next chapter. To make assurance double sure, we can safeguard the climber by sinking a bottomless box of thin wood into the ground before filling it with prepared soil; the wood will decay in time, but meanwhile the roots of the climber will have become strong enough to fight for themselves.[1] During the first year or two the real danger is not root competition, but drought, so that climbers so planted must be copiously watered until established.

An alternative method is to pick a spot just beyond the extremity of one of the lower branches of the host-tree and, having prepared the ground, plant a long and stout pole, slanting slightly inwards to the tree. The selected branch is tied to the pole and the climber then climbs up, maybe with a little assistance. Do this in the leeward side of the prevailing wind and avoid any tree with whippy branches that will flog about in any high wind. Not a suitable method for climbing roses.

Shrubs. We have discussed the problems of trees as hosts. Much more suitable to our purposes as a rule, however, are shrubs, whether evergreen or deciduous. These, of course, will accommodate only the less rampant climbers, but they will do so uncommonly well, and will need almost no attention beyond the sort of pruning appropriate to each.

Virtually any shrub of fairly tall stature and ample breadth will suit, but it is usually most satisfying to marry a late-flowering climber with an early flowering shrub or the other way round and one would not, I hope, smother shrubs grown specially for the charm and grace of their foliage, such as the Japanese maples. The dark bottle-green of a holly, the taller the better, makes a stunning backdrop for clematis, so does a big laurustinus, which is of no great attraction after the winter is over. Lilac, the Judas tree, cotoneasters, philadelphus, witch hazel, forsythia, weigela, the Syrian hibiscus, the ceanothus and eucryphias are all excellent hosts. On these we could use for preference the solanums or the climbers that hang on by coiled or curling tendrils; of these the clematis is the sovereign choice, but in the Gulf Stream counties one can use the engaging, daisyform mutisia or the orange funnels of bignonia. We have to be a bit careful about honeysuckles, whose twining stems may perhaps throttle the stems of less vigorous shrubs – hence the corkscrew walking-sticks cut from hedges.

Provided that the host shrub is a well-established plant, no great difficulty arises in choosing the spot to plant its mate. Normally

[1] *Wall Shrubs and Hardy Climbers*, by W. J. Bean, 1939.

this will be a little beyond the extremity of the foliage and on the north side. If the shrub continues to grow and invade the root area the climber, I doubt if much harm will be done, unless the climber becomes completely smothered.

Hedges. With a good deal of circumspection, a few climbers can be put to work to enliven a hedge. The first problem is root competition, which can be dealt with by the bottomless-box method. The second problem is to reconcile the seasons of pruning both hedge and climber. Honeysuckle, the jasmine-scented mandevilla and trachelospermum, some clematis and roses of various styles are available to us. Roses will not get in the way seriously on hedges that have to be pruned repeatedly during the season, such as hawthorn and privet, but clematis and honeysuckle need care in the choice of the right varieties. Morning Glory is a natural-born hedge climber.

Two safe hedges for the climbers are the Syrian hibiscus (*H. syriacus*) which needs virtually no pruning at all, and the laurels, which normally need none but a little clipping of extremities with secateurs.

However, a better opportunity still is offered to the twining climbers where one inherits from a non-gardener some shabby and neglected old hedge, which ought otherwise to be grubbed up. We can escape that tough job and forget altogether about pruning the hedge by considering it merely as a ready-made host for the climbers of our desiring, not bothering whether its shoots become twisted by the stem-clasping grip of honeysuckle and the like, so that before a year has passed we shall possess quite a new kind of hedge. We can make it an evergreen one with the rather commonplace but amorously scented Japanese honeysuckle (*Lonicera japonica*) or, where the climate allows, with the beautiful, lustrous, jasmine-scented trachelospermum and mandevilla.

CHAPTER 3

DOWN TO EARTH

Preparation – Planting – Pruning

THE cultivation of climbing plants does not materially differ from that of any other style of plant. Elsewhere[1] I have written on this subject at some length and therefore shall not repeat in detail what I have there said, but shall merely outline the courses to be followed. Moreover, I must assume for the purposes of this book that the reader is not a complete beginner.

As in nearly all gardening, the first requirement is good drainage. If the water table lies within 15 inches of ground level, the outlook will not be promising and for many plants it should be much lower. Thus if the ground does not release excess water naturally, artificial drainage must be provided.

Assuming that, as is usual, each climber is to be planted separately, mark out a hole not less than 4 feet square – five is better – or the equivalent of that area. Very often there is only a narrow bed between a house wall and a path, but, provided the bed is not less than about 2 feet wide, this will not bother the average plant, for it will be quite happy to run its feet under the path, on the strict understanding that no penetrating weed killer, such as sodium chlorate, is used on the path.

The majority of climbers and wall plants – there are exceptions, as in the Passion-flower – do their duty best only when provided with a soil that is at once rich in plant food, fairly porous but retentive of moisture.

Nothing is richer in natural food than good, "fat" loam and, if you are fortunate enough to have soil of this nature, not exhausted by the roots of plants already growing there, all that has to be done is

[1] In *The Small Garden,* now available in the Pan paperback edition, but to be superseded in a year or so by *The Modern Small Garden.*

to dig over the plot two spits deep (18 to 20 inches) by the process of double-digging, breaking up the bottom spit with the fork and keeping it at its own level and then returning the top spit. Half a barrow-load of decayed leaf-mould of oak or beech, or alternatively of *damp* peat, mixed with the top, will do a power of good.

When, as often occurs at the footings of house walls because of builders' operations, the soil is not of this nature, it must be enriched, with such exceptions as will be noticed later. To do so, turn in about four bucketfuls of cow manure (not too fresh) into the bottom spit; some of it may be allowed to lie on the top of this spit, but on the whole it is better to keep animal manure out of the top spit, as direct contact with the roots of young plants can sometimes be damaging.

Into the top spit incorporate liberal quantities of the decayed leaf-mould or damp peat that I have just mentioned and mix in a dusting of good *organic* fertilizer, such as Eclipse, which is made from fish refuse, or Maxicrop, which is processed seaweed (it is available in liquid or granular form).

In the absence of manure, compost can be used, if you have been clever enough to make it so well that all weed seeds have been burnt up. Compost can be laid into both spits, but I prefer, because of the weed-seed risk, to keep it a good 4 inches below the surface.

Other available materials are the composted sewage sold by many local authorities and "composted manure" advertised commercially. These seem usually to be reliable and the local authorities' stuff good, but all seem to contain a certain amount of lime and should not be used for lime-hating plants (of which there are few in our field of study). Of the commercial brands of composted manure, I have found Stimgro reliable.

Special soils need special treatment. Sandy ones need an extra bulk of organic stuff, and there is nothing better for them than to add liberal quantities of old, chopped-up turf to the peat and the manure and/or compost; the turf, in cubes of about 2 inches, should go into both spits, but not nearer to the surface than some 4 inches, or you are likely to have a good crop of grass.

Chalky soils are difficult, especially if the chalk is very near the surface. Here the treatment is much the same as for sand, but hacking up the stuff with a pick is a tough job. The dug-in matter rapidly breaks down in chalk and must subsequently be renewed by heavy annual mulches.

In heavy clays there is less need for bulky manures or composts, but peat will be of tremendous value in improving the physical structure of the soil. In addition to its other virtues, peat has the effect of liberating acids that precipitate the clay colloids, thus reducing the obstinate, sticky quality and, by holding the clay particles apart, gives the young roots of the plant an easy start. Use it therefore as liberally as you like and as your purse allows. In my younger days peat was almost given away, but unfortunately most of it today is in the hands of big business, with the inevitable result.

If possible, do this groundwork at least a month before planting is due. Until then leave the ground alone and do not compact it.

Planting

Autumn, the earlier the better, is the most desirable time for most plants, the ground being then still warm, but moist. If the plants have not arrived by then (and they may not if you have failed to order well in advance), any time up to the end of March will suit, or later still in northern counties, provided the ground is neither frostbound nor sodden; a mere crust of surface frost, with loose, moist soil beneath, is no impediment.

To this general rule of autumn planting there are certain qualifications, largely dependent on where one lives. All plants suffer a bit of a shock on being dug up and moved, especially after a wearisome journey by British Rail. Those that suffer the sharpest are the evergreens, because they are never dormant and continue transpiring all the year. Thus one is often advised not to plant evergreens until April, or even May in the midlands and the north. I am sure that this is wise in those areas, but in the south I have always found October to be quite satisfactory for the hardier sorts, as the rains of the autumn and winter keep them well watered, which are their prime requirement, and they are thus ready to get off their mark as soon as spring arrives. Light, sandy soils particularly invite autumn planting.

Soils that are very heavy and wet in winter, however, add to the risk and grey-leaved plants are particularly susceptible to winter damp in their first year. Such evergreen shrubs as ceanothus and escallonia are best left till spring everywhere, except in the south-west. Whenever one is in doubt, the safest thing is to ask the nurseryman for spring delivery, and, in the exceptional case of the passion flower, May or even June.

Anything on the danger line of hardiness that is planted in the autumn, whether evergreen or deciduous, had better be protected in the first winter. The simplest method is to knock up a framework of sticks, fix it firmly in the ground and drape some sacking over it. Avoid putting on the sacking until frost threatens seriously and whip it off in any mild spells. Extra protection is given by some straw loosely packed inside the sacking tent. Polythene may be used in place of sacking, provided some small holes are pierced in it. Deciduous plants that may funk the first winter can be deeply quilted with leaves, held in place by a cage of wire netting.

However, we are getting a little ahead of our subject and have not yet put our plants in the ground. Should they arrive at an unpropitious time, particularly when the ground is either frozen hard or sodden with rain, put the parcel, partially opened, into a shed or garage and wrap the roots up well. Provided you have gone to a decent nursery they will be safe for anything up to a fortnight and perhaps more, especially if the roots are kept moist and the foliage of evergreens sprayed with water daily.

On the other hand, if the soil is in suitable shape but a delay in planting is imposed by some other factor, get the plants out of their parcel as soon as possible and heel them in temporarily in some vacant ground, with the roots well covered with earth and well watered.

When all is ready, examine the roots. Cut back any that are damaged with a sloping cut on the underside of the plant and cut back also any that are excessively long, as is sometimes found in pot-grown plants after the coiled roots have been teased out. When the roots are very dry, soak them in water for a couple of hours or, in the case of plants that arrive in a bagged ball of soil, until the water stops bubbling, keeping the roots in their sacking meanwhile.

Without further delay make ready to plant. Where the climber is to be put against a wall, do not fall into the popular error of planting it too close to the wall. The soil at the footings of all walls dries out excessively and the plant should therefore go in at least 9 inches away from it. Many plants fail for this reason, especially honeysuckles, which have a predilection for very damp, almost boggy soils. A house of only two storeys, with deeply overhanging eaves (like mine) is even drier at the footings than others, as the architect intended.

Make the hole of rather larger circumference (though it need not necessarily be round) than the spread of the roots. Make sure that the bottom of it is not concave; indeed, the disposition of the roots may make it evident that they would like to be sitting on a little mound or saddle at the bottom of the hole. Make the depth such that the stem of the plant will be at the same depth as it was at the nursery, which is usually evidenced by the "soil mark" on the stem. This depth can be gauged by laying a cane across the hole at the ground level and offering up the plant. There are some exceptions to the general precept of planting to the soil mark, particularly the clematis, and these will be noticed in due course.

When satisfied, work a handful of bonemeal into the soil. Put in the plant, spread the roots out well, toss in some fine soil or peat, mixed with a trifle more bonemeal, to filter in between the roots, and half fill the hole with its own soil. As you proceed, you may see evidence that there will be some air pockets around the roots; if so, give the plant a little up-and-down shake.

The next requirement is to be sure that the roots are firmly seated. One is so often told that they should be "well trodden in", but this is sound practice only on light soils. What has to be guarded against is compacting the soil, which causes the passage of both air and water to be obstructed.

Now, the best of all "punners" of soil, to use a builder's term, is water. Excessive treading may also have the effect of leaving the plant in a perilous depression. Accordingly, on all but light soils, give only a light firming, with either foot or fist, and then give the roots a long, long drink. Go away for two or three hours, then add some more soil to the hole, give another moderate firming, top up the hole completely and give another long drink. Make sure that the plant is very firm and snug about its collar and finally put in a cane or other device to guide the plant to its destined host.

From now onwards the first need of the young plant, especially an evergreen one, is WATER. To hardy plants, the chief danger is not the frosts of winter, but drying east winds and the drought that may occur any time from March onwards. From that month onwards, especially in chalky and sandy soils, the plant must have a good drink at least once a week, either from heaven or from the watering can. Not little daily dribbles, but a good soaking. Keep this up, as needed, throughout the first spring and summer.

Pruning

Pruning is apt to be an alarming bogey to gardeners of limited experience, especially as the terms employed in it are not always explained. Let us therefore start with some simple definitions of the few that are necessary for our purposes

WOOD means any stem, branch, shoot or what you will.

NEW WOOD is any shoot that has grown during the current season.

OLD WOOD is any that has grown in a previous season.

A LEADER is the main stem of a plant or sometimes (as in fan-trained trees) a lateral shoot that becomes treated as one of several main stems.

A LATERAL is a side shoot from a main stem; there are also sub-laterals and so on.

A BREASTWOOD shoot is one that grows outwards from the wall (usually undesirable).

A BUD OR EYE may be either a growth bud or a flower bud; in pruning it usually means a growth bud. "Cut back laterals to two buds" and similar phrases mean: leave only two buds on the lateral, counting from its junction with its parent stem.

SUMMER PRUNING is a system that is highly profitable for flower production on some plants (e.g. wisteria and Japanese quince), as also on several fruits. It consists in a nipping back of new laterals during the summer, usually to the extent of leaving only about five leaves on the new shoot, but without touching the leaders. It is not to be confused with the much harder cutting back that we give after midsummer to those plants that have finished their flowering by then and are preparing to put out their new wood or have already begun to do so (e.g. deutzia, weigela, philadelphus). Summer pruning is best done generally over a period of weeks, not all at one go, to save the plant from excessive defoliation.

As far as we are concerned here, the main purposes of pruning are:

To induce the maximum possible display of flower or foliage.

To direct the plant to grow in any ordained direction. Thus a pyracantha, ceanothus or ivy planted below or near a window is beheaded when young to make it throw out lateral arms; for it is to be remembered that, in general, the effect of pruning is to induce new growth.

To restrain a plant from excessive growth.

The ways by which we achieve these ends vary somewhat, though they all have a generally similar basis. The rose and the clematis have their own special laws. Fortunately there are quite a lot of climbers that rarely need any attention at all, particularly the clingers, and many of the evergreen wall shrubs, such as the camellia. Whatever the plant, however, there are a few general precepts that may be laid down at the start for all:

First, if in doubt whether to prune, don't.

If in doubt whether to prune hard or lightly, prune lightly.

Always and invariably cut out all dead, diseased and feeble growth.

Cut back into clean, healthy wood that shows no discoloration.

Always cut just above an eye or bud or, when removing a whole limb, flush with its junction with another limb; leave no snag or stub. Choose an eye pointing in the desired direction, usually outward.

Dress all cuts an inch or more thick with "Arbrex".

And for goodness sake do treat yourself to one or more pairs of really good secateurs. The best I know are the Rolcut "Ambassador", which is hollow ground, the Wilkinson's "Super Sword Pruner" (both of which are of Christmas present price) and the Swiss "Felco". For thick stems, such as tough old roses, the two-handled Wilkinson or Rolcut pruner, with handles about 2 feet long, are very desirable and in extreme cases a pruning saw may be needed; after using the saw, pare the surface of the cut clean and smooth with a very sharp knife.

That is perhaps as far as one may dogmatize. Other issues, such as the extent and the timing of the pruning, are less clearly cut.

The first general intent (the clematis being in part an exception) is to build up a shapely framework suited to our purpose, such as a pyracantha hugging the wall or a wisteria with its main arms well spread out over its destined surface.

The next is to stimulate, year by year, the maximum display of flowers, leaf or berry. This will often mean the encouragement of new wood at the expense of the old by cutting back shoots that have finished flowering.

This brings us to the question: When to prune? Here we have a nice, easy guiding light provided by nature herself, its application being ruled by the time of year at which each plant flowers and is of general but not invariable validity.

Under this ordinance, plants that flower before midsummer, on wood that has developed in the previous year, are pruned immediately after they have finished flowering, and those that flower after midsummer on wood grown in the current season are pruned in winter or very early spring. Examples of the earlies are the forsythias, *Ceanothus dentatus* and *Clematis macropetala*; and of the lates, roses in general, *Ceanothus* 'Autumnal Blue' and *Clematis jackmanii.* I have taken the ceanothus and clematis examples to show that plants of the same genus may need different treatment.

Having prescribed all these ordinances, let me hasten to qualify them by adding that there are a great many plants that need no pruning at all.

CHAPTER 4

ROSES

"Horses for Courses" – Making Ready – Planting – Pruning – Maintenance – Varieties to Choose

ROSES are in a special category of their own, for they have no means of climbing other than their thorns, an apparatus which is effective only when they climb trees or when, with obvious ardour, they cling to the garments of the gardener.

However, the extraordinary versatility of the rose and its willing adaptability to all sorts of use put it in the front rank of ascending plants. It is not, of course, normally evergreen and has little charm in winter, nor, as a climber or rambler, is its floral season particularly long, with some exceptions that we shall shortly note; but its performance is sumptuous and, with a few reservations, it is bone-hardy, several varieties being the very thing for a cold north-facing wall. Among those varieties that climb, ramble, scramble or spread, there are some that adapt themselves to all sorts of purposes – shooting up house walls, cascading over pergolas, arches and sheds, scrambling up tall trees or elegantly twining round pillars. Some also make splendid floral hedges.

"Horses for Courses"

It will be as well if, right at the start, we get a clear idea of the different forms and shapes of the many roses that have an ascending habit, for the word "climber" is very ambiguous. They differ considerably in their usages and in their methods of pruning. Remorse and recrimination often follow an erroneous choice.

Ramblers. Typically, these are roses with long, thin, flexible canes, represented by such old varieties as 'Dorothy Perkins' and 'Excelsa'.

They derive largely from the wild species *Rosa wichuraiana*, which in nature grows flat on the ground with whippy shoots and small, shining leaves. Hence they are often called "Wichuraiana ramblers". Even here, however, we have to be careful about a too facile classification, for the Wichuraiana hybrids vary a good deal in their behaviour.

At one end of the scale are those of which we take 'Dorothy Perkins' as the type. Their chief characteristic is that, like raspberries, they throw out long new canes from ground level or near it, but do not flower on them until the next year. This characteristic is the key to their pruning.

A second characteristic is their susceptibility to mildew. They should *never* be planted on a wall, where they will trap all the mildew spores floating in the air, but in open situations on arches, trellises or wound round tall, wooden tripods. Even so, they will need thorough spraying.

Though no plants of any genus are more profligate with their floral gifts, many of the wichuraiana ramblers have to a large extent been displaced by newer varieties less subject to disease, but they still have their place where a country cottage atmosphere is the objective. Among these are 'Dorothy Perkins', 'Excelsa', 'Minnehaha', 'Sander's White' and 'Lady Godiva' – none of them roses to choose unless you have a special passion for them.

At the other end of the wichuraiana scale are a few varieties, notably 'Albertine', that do not behave in this way and have to be treated in the same manner as the thick-stemmed climbers. We shall note these as we go along. There are also fortunately a few that are much less prone to mildew than the 'Dorothy Perkins' class, notably the beautiful 'Emily Gray', 'Albertine', 'François Juranville', 'May Queen' and 'Thelma'.

Climbers. Though the boundaries are far from being clearly defined, the roses in this group differ from the ramblers in that (in general terms) they build up strong, thick, rigid main limbs which do not need to be cut back hard each year and which produce new canes occasionally from the ground but more often from some point higher up on the old ones. Most of these are far too strong and rigid in growth for arches, pergolas or low fences and need large walls for the display of their magnificent limbs. Among them are the big classic climbers such as 'Mermaid', 'Allen Chandler', 'Guinée', the old 'Gloire de Dijon', 'Mme Alfred Carrière' and so on.

Also among them are all those strong roses known as "climbing sports". These are climbing forms of the Hybrid Tea and the Floribunda roses grown in formal beds. They bear exactly the same flowers as their progenitors, but, unlike them, bloom once only (in June), though sometimes they throw occasional blooms afterwards. Indeed, most of the other climbers likewise bloom once only, but they do so with the utmost abandon and create magnificent spectacles if properly displayed.

Nearly all these climbers will easily reach the eaves of a small, two-floor house and many will go much higher, thus making a wonderful embellishment for the wall but creating problems of training and tying.

Pillar or **Short Climbers.** Here we have a mixed bag that contains many sumptuous roses, old and new. They are of mingled blood, not easily pigeon-holed into categories. They vary from the enchanting little 'Climbing Pompon de Paris' to twelve-footers such as 'Nymphenburg' and include several that bloom repeatedly, such as 'Golden Showers,' which never stops from June to October. In general they resist disease well. Their natural habit is as open-growing shrubs and, with such exceptions as 'Golden Showers' and 'Aloha', need a little training by the hand of man to develop a "pillar" shape. They often fill the bill as climbers on house-walls in which the windows are too close together for the more lusty climbers and are valuable in the open garden also if provided with tall and strong structures for their support. In their appropriate section we shall note the uses to which each can be put.

Tree Climbers. There are a few woodland roses that will scramble at express speed to the tops of trees 25 feet high and more, flowering for a short time in huge trusses of white flowers, copiously embalming the air with a sweet breath. They need virtually no attention. A few of the sophisticated hybrids will behave in a like manner, though less vigorously, such as 'Mme Alfred Carrière' and 'American Pillar'.

Making Ready

Elsewhere[1] I have written at some length on the cultivation of roses in general, so that here I can only adapt what has already been said to the special purposes of the ascending varieties. At the outset we

[1] *Roses for Small Gardens* (Pan Books).

may specify that the fundamental needs for growing them successfully are:

Good drainage, with the water running away freely after heavy rain;

a deeply dug, enriched soil;
plenty of sun, though some will succeed in partial shade;
plenty of water in dry periods;
protection against pests and diseases.

The rose is a marvellous trier in almost any kind of soil, but what it seems to like most is a "fat", fibrous loam slightly on the acid side (about pH 6·5). The preliminary treatment is of the utmost importance. No amount of top feeding after the roses have been planted can make good any errors or omissions below ground.

Therefore dig the ground two spits (20 inches) deep by the process of double digging. In the bottom spit incorporate chopped-up turves (say about 2 inches square) and cow or horse manure (at two bucketfuls per square yard), with some of the manure lying on the top of the bottom spit. Compost, if really well made, can be substituted for the manure.

In the top spit incorporate more chopped-up turf (keeping it a good 4 inches from the surface), plenty of peat (a barrow-load per 2 square yards) and a good sprinkling of an organic fertilizer (such as "Eclipse", "Maxicrop", hop manure or meat-and-bonemeal) to give some heart to the peat. No animal manure may be used in the top spit, but compost is good, though it should be kept 4 inches or so below the surface if it has not been made so well as to be certain that all weed seeds have been burnt up.

In light, sandy soils in which water runs away quickly and in which fertilizers are quickly washed out, the quantities of turf, manure and compost should be doubled. The same applies to chalky soils, which are the most unpropitious of all; here old turves are the sovereign diet. In heavy clays increase the peat by spreading a 2-inch layer over all and then working it in by turning over the top 4 inches with a light fork.

This preparation of the ground should, if possible, be done a good month before planting-time, which may be anything from October to March, with a strong preference for the autumn. Leave the bed rough for a week or two, so that air can get well in, then break up the surface clods with a fork, leaving all smooth, but be careful not to compact the nice, loose soil by treading on it.

Above: Clematis macropetala

Below: Plumbago capensis

Hydrangea petiolaris

For the kinds of rose that we are here considering, it will not always be necessary to dig a large bed. Where they are to be planted singly, make the prepared area not less than 4 feet by 4 feet or its equivalent. But where a whole pergola, screen or fence is to be planted, dig over the whole length of the area 4 feet wide.

Planting

Planting a rose sounds a simple enough job, but it can be done well or ill. For the varieties we are considering the first thing to do is to plant a firm stake to support the canes against the furies of the first winter, unless the rose is of a variety that has to be cut nearly down to the ground.

The next requirement is to have ready a planting mixture made of peat and meat-and-bonemeal (or, if that is not easily obtainable, ordinary bonemeal of a medium grade). Use a large handful of the meal per bucket of peat or six double handfuls per barrow.

Examine the roots. Cut away any damaged ones and shorten any that are unduly long; 15 inches is more than enough.

More often than not, you will find that the rose has been grown at the nursery with the roots all flowing in one general direction. This saves one a great deal of trouble. One has merely to dig a fan-shaped hole, about 5 inches deep where the crown of the rose is to be planted and about 8 inches deep at the extremity of the roots.

Now put in your planting mixture, about half a bucket per plant and mix it up evenly with the soil. Put in the plant so that the crown will be only just covered when the soil is returned to the hole. Fan out the roots widely, using stones to separate and fix any that have become twisted. Pour in another half-bucketful of the planting mixture (more if you like), half-fill the hole with soil and then tread the roots in firmly with your feet, the root extremities first. Finally return the remainder of the soil.

If the roots of the rose, as received, are found to be growing out in all directions, a round hole will be necessary, with a slight mound or saddle in the middle of the hole. This is a tiresome method of planting, as the hole is easily made too deep or too shallow; therefore put a cane across the centre of the hole at the true ground level and "offer up" the plant until the right depth is ensured.

Pruning

It is not easy to explain pruning in cold print. Ten minutes of practical demonstration by an old hand is better than a whole volume. However, the way begins to open up when we realize that the natural habit of the rose is constantly to put on new "wood" and for the old wood gradually to fall into the discard, turning dark, hard and barren. What the rosarian does, in principle, is to hasten this natural process, constantly encouraging new growth by amputating the old before it becomes useless.

Of roses as a whole, we may say that what we aim at is a complete change of the structure about every three years or so by annually cutting away about one-third of the growth. This holds good for only some of the ascending roses, however, for in 'Dorothy Perkins' and her like we want a completely new set of limbs every year, but, at the other end of the scale, we prune 'Mermaid' and 'Emily Gray' very little. In between are many variations, but, with such rare exceptions as those I have mentioned, all ascending roses fall readily into one or the other of the two following categories:

Prune 1. This is confined to the flexible 'Dorothy Perkins' group. When planting, amputate all the canes to within 15 inches of the ground. This seemingly callous treatment is most important and must not be funked. It means that you will have no flowers in the first season, but that you will get nice, long, new canes, which will bloom madly the next. Note that the flower trusses will grow out laterally from the canes.

In subsequent years, cut the canes that have flowered hard back in August or September, to foster the growth of further new ones that should by now be evident. Where the new growth sprouts liberally from the ground (as in the upper sketch in Fig. 7) cut the flowered canes clean down to the earth, leaving no stumps.

If growth does not come actually from the ground, but from a point low down or half-way up an old stem, as often in 'American Pillar', 'Crimson Conquest', and 'François Juranville', cut down to that point. On the other hand, if too few basal shoots should appear, retain the strongest old canes and prune the flowered *laterals* to within 3 inches of its parent stem.

Varieties to which this "Prune 1" treatment applies are: 'Dorothy Perkins', 'Excelsa', 'Crimson Shower', 'Crimson Conquest', 'François

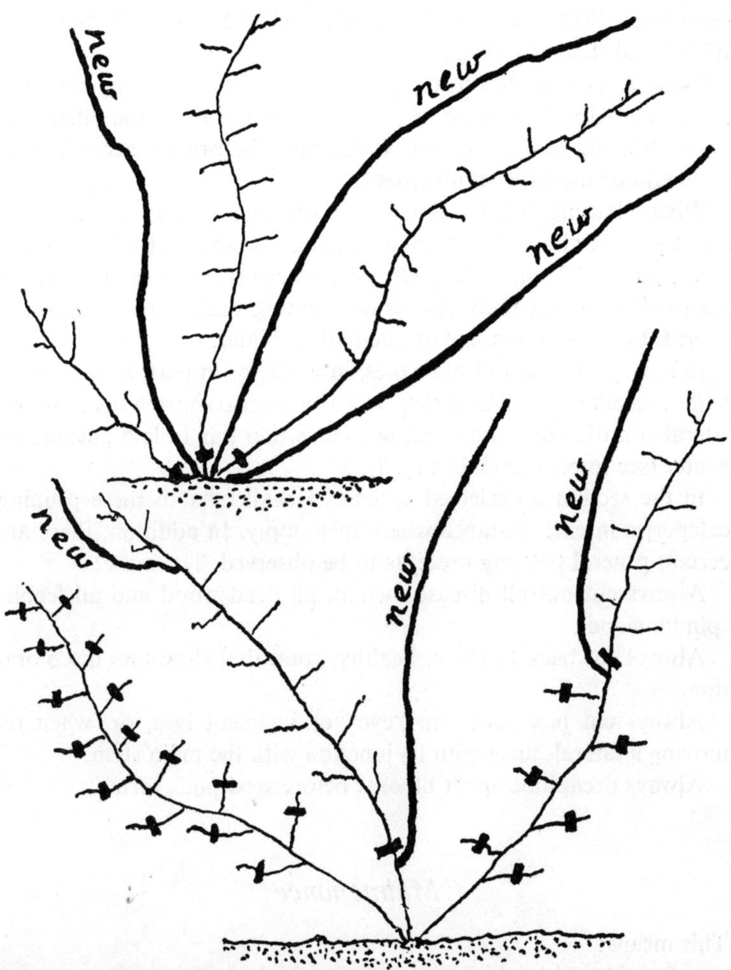

FIG. 7. Pruning rambling and climbing roses. The "new wood" grown in the current season is shown by the long, thick lines, and the old, flowered wood by thin ones. The very short, thick marks are the pruning points. *Top:* A rambler of the 'Dorothy Perkins' habit, with all old, flowered canes cut to the ground (unless no new canes). *Below:* On other ramblers and on climbers in general, prune according to the amount of new wood available to replace the old; on old wood that is retained, shorten the laterals.

Juranville', 'May Queen', 'Mary Wallace', 'Minnehaha', 'Sander's White' and 'Lady Godiva'.

Prune 2. This applies to the great majority of the strong climbers and to the Albertine group of ramblers, but not to all the pillar and short climbing sorts, a few of which must be pruned according to the methods used for shrub roses.

When planting, lightly cut back the tips by about 3 inches. Subsequently leave the main canes untouched for the first two or three years, so as to build up a strong framework, and confine pruning to clearing out weak shoots and cutting back the old, flowered *laterals* by about one-third or one-half in winter.

In later years, cut out old canes, in whole or in part, *in proportion to the amount of new shoots that have grown*; also shorten the flowered laterals on old canes retained, as before. Do this in late autumn or winter (see lower sketch in Fig. 7).

In the section on selected varieties I shall refer to these pruning categories in each instance where they apply. In addition, there are certain general pruning precepts to be observed. These are:

Always cut out all diseased wood, all dead wood and all feeble, spindly wood.

Always cut back to clean, healthy wood that shows no discoloration.

Always cut just above an "eye" or incipient bud, or, when removing a lateral, flush with its junction with the main stem.

Always decapitate spent blooms before seed pods form.

Maintenance

This means:

- Pruning, with which we have already dealt.
- Training and tying.
- Spraying.
- Deadheading.
- Watering.

Training and tying. On walls, fences, screens, pergolas, outbuildings and so on, the first aim is to spread the main limbs out well, while they are young and fairly flexible. The strong climbers, in particular, profit from being led out more or less horizontally, an attitude that encourages them to throw out plenty of good, strong lateral growths; left to grow upright they tend to flower mainly in tufts at the top, especially the climbing sports.

The wichuraiana ramblers and others with thin, flexible canes can be twined round tall pillars, bent over arches, fanned out on open screens or, in a free-and-easy garden, left to ramble at will over shrubs, tumble down banks or behave in any other light-hearted manner.

Tying is a job that needs fairly frequent attention from July onwards. On any sort of wooden or wire support all that is needed is string that is not only strong and thick but also soft. "Tarred string" is acceptable, but rather harsh. The spools of thin, green stuff are no good for this sort of job. On brick or concrete walls one has first to provide something to which the string can be tied. This can be by any of the means described in Chapter 2.

Spraying. Like all roses, the climbers and ramblers must be sprayed against insect pests and against fungal diseases. Most pests are effectively kept at bay by spraying with a systemic insecticide, such as "Toprose", "Abol X" or Murphy's "Systemic Insecticide". Spray first early in May and again in July if it should be necessary. I have not seen a greenfly on my roses for years.

Fungus diseases – mildew, black spot and rust – are another and more troublesome matter. The simplest course is to use a combined spray, such as Pan Britannica's Rose Disease Spray or Murphy's Rose Fungicide, starting in May and repeating every fortnight (yes!) until September.

Deadheading. This means beheading the flowers as soon as they are spent, in order to stop the plant from putting its vigour into setting seed. On the classes of rose that we are dealing with here it is sufficient to snip off the incipient seed pod (or bunch thereof) just above the second leaf beneath it, until pruning-time in autumn or winter.

Watering. Never leave roses more than ten days without water. In the absence of rain, turn on the hose for not less than half an hour, using a soft, gentle mist-forming sprinkler or, better still, the Supplex style flat hose with minute holes all along its length. Roses on walls need more than others and you should give them a good drink every week if nature does not do so.

Varieties to Choose

I give here a short selection of varieties that I can recommend for various uses, cutting out those that have bad habits such as 'Dorothy Perkins' and those that are commonplace, such as 'Chaplin's Pink Climber'. Jolly they may be, but there are so many that far excel them.

STRONG CLIMBERS

The 'Prune 2' rules apply to all these except 'Mermaid', the Banksian Rose, 'Cupid', 'Mme Alfred Carrière' and 'Lawrence Johnson'.

Allen Chandler. Large, vivid, crimson-scarlet HT flowers, good enough for cutting, liberally borne on a plant of great vigour that may throw out canes 18 feet long. One of the very best for a large house wall, but not a red-brick one. Makes a magnificent and prolonged display at the end of May, continues to bear a few flowers and has another outburst in the autumn. One of the most successful roses for a cold north wall. Unsuitable for confined spaces.

Banksian Roses. Lady Banks's Rose is the wild white *Rosa banksiae* 'Alba-plena' and its yellow form is *R.b.* 'Lutea'. Both are sumptuous climbers and greatly to be cherished by anyone who has a tall house with a large, warm south wall in the warmest counties only. They will grow 40 feet high (much higher in warmer lands) and flower in spring. When happy they bloom in great profusion and they do so on *sub*-laterals. The white one is deliciously scented, the yellow one less so but more beautiful.

Beyond removal of the dead flower trusses, no pruning should be done for the first six years, when some of the very oldest wood should be cut out, but taking great care not to lose any strong young canes growing out of the old.

The Banksian roses also make magnificent tree climbers where the climate is really warm.

Climbing Sports. There are a lot of these, most being sports for HT bushes, but a few from floribundas. Nearly all are good, but the following have perhaps the best all-round value.

CLIMBING CAROLINE TESTOUT. A Victorian beauty, whose large, full-bosomed flowers in deep, warm pink belie the threatening asptec of her fierce armament of thorns. It has a good repeat flowering

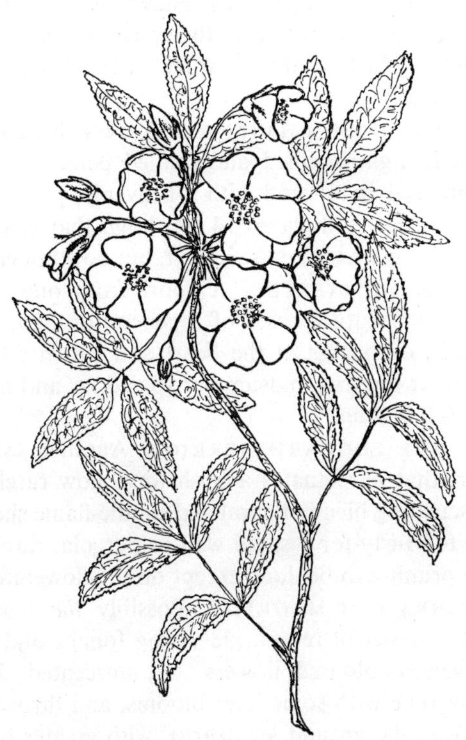

FIG. 8. *Rosa banksiae.*

after the first splendid display, but not much scent. It is of tremendous vigour, reaching anything up to 20 feet.

CLIMBING CRIMSON GLORY. This fine sport, in deep, dusky, velvety red, is endowed with a wonderful scent. Of modest stature for this class of rose, it seldom exceeds 10 feet and is not suitable for a red-brick wall.

CLIMBING ENA HARKNESS. The bush 'Ena Harkness' is one of the very top of our bedding roses, with warmly scented blooms of rich scarlet-crimson. Its climbing sport carries the same beautiful roses 14 feet high up a house wall, but preferably not a red brick. It often has a second crop.

CLIMBING ETOILE DE HOLLANDE. Between the two wars 'Etoile de Hollande' was the undisputed queen of dark red HT roses. Her climbing sport continues happily to remind us of that wonderful, dark red with the black-velvet flush, the sweet breath – and the nodding head. Possibly the best of these three dark red sports, extending its arms to 16 feet.

CLIMBING MME ABEL CHATENAY. A very beautiful rose of exquisite form in tightly coiled and quilled petals of warm pink, produced in great abandon and with a heavenly, penetrating scent. A very desirable rose, with canes 14 feet long, that clambered over and round an arbour where we used to sit, but now not easy to get.

CLIMBING MME BUTTERFLY. A sport from one of the most famous and most beautiful roses of a generation ago, with coiled, pale pink petals, deepening at the heart and a rich scent. It often bears flowers after the first midsummer splendour and may produce canes nearly 20 feet long.

CLIMBING MME EDOUARD HERRIOT. Another example of a climbing sport that perpetuates a bush form now rarely seen. The colour is a fascinating blend of coral and candle-flame shades, unique in roses. Not too lusty for a small wall or pergola, rarely exceeding 12 feet. Little pruning to be done except on the flowered laterals.

CLIMBING MRS SAM MCGREDY. Possibly *the* finest climbing sport, with its wonderful red-purple young foliage and its prodigal eruption of sunset-coloured flowers, but unscented. It begins to flower in early June with some later blooms, and throws out strong new growth from the ground, or near it, with greater freedom than any other of its kind, reaching to 14 feet.

CLIMBING SHOT SILK. The modest little charmer of the HT beds, once in the very forefront of bedding roses, richly fragrant, throws out strong arms up to 12 feet in length, richly festooned with shining orange lamps.

Cupid. A gorgeous rose of peach-pink, very large, almost single and richly scented, followed by huge orange hips, carried on fiercely barbed canes that may grow to about 14 feet. It flowers in July only and needs a warm wall facing south or west, its hardiness being doubtful. No pruning is needed beyond the shortening of flowered laterals and the occasional removal of decadent old canes.

Elegance. A climber of great vigour, with strong, thick stems, adorned with stylishly modelled flowers of clear gold, long and pointed, which are displayed at midsummer, with some blooms later. Prone to the malady of die-back, but produces strong new shoots with abundance, extending to 16 feet.

Gloire de Dijon. This grand old rose still holds its own after more than a century and is one of the best for a cold north wall. The buff flowers, orange at the heart, breathe a sublime aroma and there are nearly always some in bloom throughout the summer. It will reach nearly 20 feet but you must get it only from leading specialist rose nurseries.

Guinée. A superlative rose with a character all its own. It is the darkest dark-red in the garden, its stylish HT blooms heavily dusted with a sooty black. It has a rich, warm scent and blooms a second time with modest freedom. It branches freely and is splendid for walls other than those of red brick. It grows to 15 feet.

High Noon. Growing (in my experience) to about 11 feet, this well-named rose bears clear, bright yellow, pointed buds, like little lamps, which look lovely against the sky or a red wall. The flowers have a clean, fresh scent, are good enough for cutting, begin to appear in early June and go on more or less continuously but not with abandon. Its fault is its sparse foliage, so that its naked lower limbs should be decently screened by some bushy plant or twined round by a pale blue clematis.

Lawrence Johnson. Semi-double flowers of bright, gleaming yellow of charming informal style, richly scented, clothing a vigorous frame that grows to 30 feet. A connoisseur's rose that begins to flower in June luxuriantly. Repeats intermittently all the summer. Prune as for 'Mermaid'.

Mermaid. Acclaimed by many as the finest of all climbing roses (strongly challenged by 'Albertine'). 'Mermaid' has tremendous vigour and its far-reaching arms, sharply barbed and decorated with stylish foliage that is almost evergreen, may stretch out for 25 feet. The canary flowers are of beautiful quality, large, single and ornamented with a prominent boss of amber stamens. They are sterile.

'Mermaid' hates being moved, must be supplied by the nursery in a pot and usually sulks for the first season. The wood is brittle and attempts to train it should be done cautiously while the stems are still young. The plant does not seem to be frost-hardy in the coldest counties, but elsewhere flowers almost as well on a north wall as on a sunny one. No pruning is needed beyond cutting out decadent wood as the plant ages.

Mme Alfred Carrière. An old rose not in the front row of glamour but of much merit and great vigour, able to reach the eaves of a moderate-sized house or (as in a former garden of mine) 18 feet high into the branches of trees. The flowers are white, with a pink blush on their cheeks, and they have a refreshing scent. One of the best roses for a north wall.

Mme Grégoire Staechelin. This is a superlative rose of the most refined beauty and lively, refreshing scent. The beautifully coiled flowers, in tones of pale and deep pink, are of romantic elegance and are produced with prodigal abandon, accompanied by glossy foliage, on strong, thick limbs that may extend to 20 feet. Alack, apart from a few late blooms, it flowers only in June.

Paul's Lemon Pillar. An unique rose this. Very large, beautifully sculptured flowers of sumptuous quality and scent are borne (at midsummer only) on strong arms that may extend to 16 feet. The name is a little deceptive, for the colour is nearly white, with only a hint of lemon, but deepening to a delightful greeny-lemon in the heart. Best on a warm wall.

Souvenir de Claudius Denoyel. One of the loveliest of dark red roses, its crimson petals lightly dusted in sooty black and enriching the garden with an exquisite scent. It blooms magnificently at midsummer and breaks out again in autumn, with occasional flowers in between. One of the top choices, it will adorn a wall for 16 feet.

PILLAR OR SHORT CLIMBING ROSES

These are for use on pillars up to about 9 feet high or as short climbers on walls, outhouses, fences, pergolas and so on. They also make splendid free-growing bushes in gardens that have the room to spare, especially 'Nyphenburg'.

Pruning. With the exception of 'Thelma' and 'The New Dawn', these need rather more pruning than the strong climbers. They should be treated in the manner of shrub roses, cutting back old flowered wood to selected buds in winter and encouraging its frequent renewal by strong new canes.

Climbing Pompon de Paris. This endearing little rose has a character and a charm all its own. Small, pale pink pompoms, such as children used to wear on their party-dress shoes, are sprinkled along slim, wiry but sharply prickled stems that are clothed with the daintiest foliage which matches their miniature elegance. It starts blooming in late May and repeats from time to time throughout the season. Maximum height, about 7 feet. For a slender pillar or post or almost any other use except a large wall (especially not a red brick one).

Danse du Feu (known as 'Spectacular' in the United States). A dramatic rose that bursts out into an exuberant display of large, deep orange-scarlet blossoms that may well take one's breath away in June. What is more, it goes on blooming more or less continuously until the autumn. A first choice where brilliant colour is the need. It grows to perhaps 12 feet and is of broadly bushy habit with fairly pliable arms. For walls (but perhaps not house-walls where the windows are close together), pergolas, arches and screens; hardly for pillars, though often called a "pillar rose".

Golden Showers. No rose so fully justifies the epithet of "perpetual flowering" as this one, for it really does bloom continuously from early June until the frost, constantly thrusting up new canes crowned with shapely, golden and scented flowers on erect stems that are good enough to cut. The habit of the plant is erect and narrow, so that it can be planted on a wall between windows or as a pillar or in an awkward corner that needs to be filled. Not suitable for arches. Seldom exceeds 8 feet.

Leverkusen. A modern short climber. The flowers are pale gold, opening from pointed buds to large, semi-double, fresh-scented blossoms borne on long stems, set off by handsome foliage. It blooms in summer and autumn, with an occasional specimen in between. The plant will reach about 10 feet, with a bushy, free-branching habit that makes it suitable for a pillar, and it is sufficiently flexible to train as one wills.

Maigold. Apart from its other qualities, this is a good rose for covering up any object that needs to be obscured, for it has abundant foliage of glossy texture. It blooms in late May, well before most others of its kind, with flowers that are bronze in the bud, opening to buff, and carrying a rich scent. About 10 feet or so, with conveniently pliable canes.

Meg. A charming short climber, bearing large, pink-and-apricot, few-petalled blooms that have a light fragrance. Of bushy, branching habit, growing to about 8 feet, it is rather broad for a pillar, but is excellent on any wall, fence or pergola. Not many flowers after July.

New Dawn. A small, shell-pink rose of tender and informal charm, deliciously scented and accompanied by attractive foliage. Its main display is at the end of June but thereafter it is seldom out of bloom. Dense and twiggy in habit, its most impressive use is as an informal hedge, but it does exceedingly well also as a broad pillar or against a fence or outhouse wall. Seldom grows more than 8 feet high, though reported to go much higher. Limit pruning to shortening laterals in winter and cutting out decadent wood when necessary.

Nyphenburg. Perhaps the most enchanting of the newer "perpetual" roses and of great value to gardeners for the variety of uses to which it can be put. Of hybrid musk parentage, its beautifully formed flowers are salmon tinted with gold, richly scented, and are poised in long-stemmed clusters, which the genus of the plant produces almost continuously throughout the summer. Its limbs, which may extend to 12 feet, are very strong yet pliable enough for us to bend to our uses, so that we may plant it on a house or other tall wall, a pergola, or covering sheds or over broad arches, which it will transform into floral arbours.

Paul's Scarlet Climber. An old favourite that still holds its own despite its lack of scent, its attractions never staling from familiarity. A very easy rose that blooms only once but does so for a long time. For a wall, fence or screen with canes well fanned out; not for arches and scarcely as a pillar. Does not often exceed 12 feet, but may go further.

Thelma. This is a pretty, coral-pink wichuraiana rambler, but I place it here because it is particularly suitable for twining round a pillar, growing no more than 9 feet. However, it does well also on a fence, outhouse, etc. It has a faint, sweet scent and is almost thornless. Prune as for 'New Dawn'.

RAMBLERS

With the possible exception of 'Albertine', none of the roses in this list is really to be recommended for growing on walls or fences. Pergolas, arches and open lattice-work are their more fitting situations, where they are less likely to be stricken with mildew. A few of the laxer sorts look splendid cascading over a terrace wall or down a bank. Except for 'Zéphirine Drouhin' and 'Kathleen Harrop', all burst out into one magnificent display and are then over.

I omit the commonplace sorts, such as 'American Pillar' and 'Dorothy Perkins'.

"Prune 1" applies to most varieties, the exceptions being noted.

Albertine. A superlative garden rose, easily the finest of the ramblers and among the first of all roses of no-matter-what class. Delightful, informal, sweetly scented, coppery-pink flowers smother the whole plant, which is of great vigour, branching freely and sharply thorned. Indeed, it makes such a dense and thorny thicket that one must consider its position and employment with care. A tall screen or long pergola are perhaps best, allowing it in part to behave with natural freedom, merely guiding the main stems in the desired direction. The canes, which may go to 16 feet on a wall are pliant when young but soon become very thick and rigid. Prune 2.

AMETHYST. See 'Rose-Marie Viaud'.

Crimson Conquest. A typical lax-limbed rambler, bearing deep scarlet flowers with a black flush, of miniature HT form, and a warm scent that makes it delightful to walk under when trained over an arch. Flowers profusely in mid-June, but only once. Goes to 14 feet. Prune 1 as far as allowed by the development of new growth, which is not always directly from the base after the first few years.

Crimson Showers. Another typical crimson rambler, scentless, but of value for its late and long flowering, which is from late July till the end of August. For arch, pergola, screen, or wound round a pillar – 14 feet. Prune 1.

Emily Gray. A very vigorous rambler with beautiful, gleaming, almost evergreen foliage and large, nearly single blossoms of a warm golden-buff and some scent. The flowers are not borne with great exuberance but occur throughout the season occasionally after the main display. For screen, fence, pergola or large arch and possibly for a house-wall; too vigorous for a pillar, its canes growing up to 18 feet long. Leave unpruned the first year or two, then Prune 2, but very lightly.

Easlea's Golden Rambler. Another rambler distinguished by the beauty of its foliage, which is a rich, glossy, olive green, as well as by its delightful flowers, which are large, red in the bud, opening to gold and borne on laterals, but only at midsummer. Rarely exceeds 12 feet and is suitable for pillars, arches, pergolas, fences, etc. Do not prune until three to four years old, then prune laterals only as for "Prune 2".

François Juranville. Deep fawn-pink, lusciously scented flowers that resemble those of 'Albertine' are borne on thin, very supple canes of exceptional vigour, extending more than 20 feet long. A once-only performer, but a valuable rose for many purposes – scrambling over outhouses, along pergolas and screens, but not pillars or small arches. A good tree climber. Reluctant to throw new canes from the base, but innumerable long shoots appear annually from higher up on the main stems. The pruning treatment is thus a modified "Prune 1"; take advantage of any strong new shoots that may occur low down and cut other old canes back to any strong new shoots to suit your purpose.

Kathleen Harrop. A sport from 'Zéphirine Drouhin', slightly less vigorous and having flowers of a desirable shell-pink.

May Queen. Obtainable from only a few nurseries, this is of greater merit than many that are better known. The typical rambler-style flowers are lilac-pink with a fresh, clean scent and are borne on supple arms, 15 feet long, densely clothed with apple-green foliage that makes it admirable for screening. It blooms early in June and is suitable for arches, screens, pergolas and perhaps for pillars.

Rose-Marie Viaud (Also known as 'Amethyst'). To people who want "something different" this may have some appeal. The flowers are approximately amethyst or pale violet, fading to lilac-grey, borne in large trusses, but unfortunately the display is short. The foliage is dense and useful for screening and it is almost thornless. To 16 feet.

Violette. Another variety for those who want "something different" and more attractive in my opinion than 'Rose-Marie Viaud'. The small flowers are deep purple, carried in large trusses, fading to a mauve-grey. Thornless, but unscented. To 12 feet or so.

Zéphirine Drouhin. Let not its exotic name put you off this charming and useful Bourbon rose. None is more continuously in bloom from June to October, few are more richly scented and, to the confusion of the poets, its slender arms are innocent of thorns. If you are one of those who are touchy about its old-fashioned carmine-pink blossoms, you can grow its daughter 'Kathleen Harrop' instead. Of upright carriage, Zéphirine seldom extends much higher than 10 feet, so is ideal as a pillar rose, but may also be trained over a narrow arch or grown as an open bush. Because of their scent and their lack of thorns, both are excellent roses for growing beside a door, provided that the wall is not of red brick. Unfortunately they fall easy prey to the spores of mildew, but are worth looking after.

TREE CLIMBERS

The following are selected species and varieties of roses that will climb anything from 20 to 40 feet up into trees. The species roses are all white, with very large trusses of marvellous, pervading scent, but are rather quickly over. Dig out a hole near the trunk of the host-tree not less than four foot square, enriching the ground liberally.

Rosa noisettiana
R. longicuspis
R. multiflora 'Gentiliana'
R. filipes 'Kiftsgate' (extremely vigorous)
'Mme Alfred Carrière'
'François Juranville'
'American Pillar'

CHAPTER 5

CLEMATIS

Its Nature and Needs – Planting – Servicing – Display – Pruning – A Choice of Clematis Varieties

IF the wisteria is the king of climbers, as it may well claim to be, the clematis is no doubt the queen. Yet it has no petals, its beauty residing in the brilliance of its sepals and often in the boss of stamens that they enfold. Wonderful in its range of colour, richly flowerful, adaptable to many uses and usually modest of stature, the clematis is an ideal climber which is as appropriate to the cottager's plot as to his lord's demesne.

Yet it has to be admitted that the clematis is not the easiest of plants to establish and to make prosper. No ivy she. No "plant and forget". She is a mistress that has to be wooed and she may jilt you even after two years courtship; thereafter, however, she is likely to be yours for life.

Two, and normally two only, problems beset the gardener. One is the pruning problem, which can be the very devil if you allow it to become so, but which will be discussed more hopefully in the appropriate section.

The other is the mysterious disease known as "wilt". When stricken by this disease the whole plant suddenly collapses, for reasons that are so far imperfectly known to the boffins of horticulture. You may order your plants from the most irreproachable nurseryman, but there can be no guarantee that, by whatever means it may have been raised, it will not suddenly pass out.

However, wilt attacks only the large-flowered hybrids (which are the most popular ones) and it occurs only on young plants; the menace is most threatening in the first year after receipt from the nursery, but it may continue to linger for another two years, when, having obeyed every command in the book, you may see a fine plant which seems to be the picture of health suddenly give up the ghost.

Schizophragma integrifolia

The 'lobster claw', *Clianthus puniceus*

Research into the disease is in hand and Mr Christopher Lloyd tells me it is now found to be due to a fungus originating in dead tissue. One precaution to take, therefore, is to gather up all dead wood and leaves and burn them.

I have put the worst side of the case first, so that it shall be looked squarely in the face.

Clematis are expensive, but if you were to ask me whether they are worth the risk, I should say Yes immediately. I have grown a good many in my time and have had my share of losses, but the successes have made me forget them. When properly grown and trained they are a marvellous enrichment to the garden's third dimension. People whose conception of a clematis is restricted to a tangled mop precariously strung up on a wall by a single nail have no idea what splendour can be achieved by a little preliminary care – and it is the preliminaries that are the most important.

Its Nature and Needs

The clematis belongs to the group that I have called the twiners. It embraces its host by ingeniously curling its long leaf-stalks firmly round the waiting arms. The various species and hybrids open to our choice can provide floral embellishment for six months or more from April, when the enchanting species *alpina* and *macropetala* begin to open their pendant bells.

Their colour range embraces yellow, white and every tint of mauve or purple from almost true blue to almost true red. The flowers are usually single, but some doubles are available for those who like them. A few wild species or varieties and forms of them are grown in our gardens, producing masses of small flowers (and these are the least liable to wilt), but the majority that we grow are large-flowered hybrids – what may (optionally) be called "cultivars" in the new formalized jargon.

The seed heads that follow the flowers of the climbers are of ingenious and delightful design, resembling a woman's well-coiffeured head, often with golden or silvery tints, and sometimes almost as beautiful as the flowers, as in the spun silk of *C. tangutica*. There is variety in the vigour of the clematis also. Whereas the average height may be said to be about 12 feet, *C. montana*, the "virgin's bower", will clamber 35 feet into a tree, but 'Hagley Hybrid', 'Lasurstern' and 'Mme Edouard André' – three of the most beautiful hybrids – seldom stretch higher than 8 feet or so. The species or varieties one orders must therefore be matched to their intended purposes.

In its natural state, as may be seen in our native *Clematis vitalba* (which is "Traveller's Joy" or "Old Man's Beard" when draped with its mantle of fluffy seed heads), the clematis grows in semi-woodland in lime-bearing soils, often in moist places and often above chalk, scrambling over bushes and hedges and up aloft into the branches of trees. The trees and bushes provide shade at ground level and an annual mulch of leaves over the roots. Let us see how we can apply these factors to the other species and varieties of clematis in their cultivated state.

In short terms the main needs of the clematis in our garden therefore are:

a soil rich in organic matter, well drained,
quantities of water,
cool shade for the roots,
light, but not necessarily direct sunlight, for the head.

What, you may ask, about the lime or chalk? For generations it has been a firmly held belief that lime in some form was natural and necessary. Today there is not the same emphasis and specialists themselves disagree. It is perfectly clear that clematis do extremely well in acid or neutral soils, as I myself can testify, but what is not so certain is whether they do better still with a little lime in their diet.

Mr Pennell and Mr Fisk are pro-lime at 4 ounces and 6 ounces per square yard respectively, but Mr Christopher Lloyd says it is quite unnecessary. I, having uo scientific pretentions, am entirely neutral in the matter and I think that the clematis is also, except in the very sour old soils that are sometimes to be found in the gardens of London and some other big cities, where lime is surely needed.

So do what you like about lime, but be sure to give the soil the full treatment ordained in Chapter 3. A plot 3 foot square will probably be big enough for clematis, but 4 feet is more to my liking. Since the clematis is a hard drinker, sandy soils are unpropitious, so if your soil is of that sort add all the bulky organic matter you can, particularly the chopped-up turves, which are the best treatment I know for sandy soils.

In choosing a site, the example of nature must be copied; a cool, shady root run must be provided. When the clematis is intended to ramble over a large shrub (its most charming manifestation) the requirement is met by planting it on the northerly side of its intended host. When it is intended to adorn a screen, arch or pergola, one or two small bushes should be planted on its southerly quarters to act as sunshades. Suitable examples are the Kurume azaleas, dwarf rhododendrons such as 'Carmen' and heathers of the stature of 'George Rendall' and 'Brightness' or, in acid soils, the gilded halimium, the shrubby species of potentilla and, when they have developed into nice bushy shrublets, the lavenders and helianthemums. Larger shrubs will, of course, also serve well.

When, however, the clematis is under orders to climb a wall, some extra precautions must be taken. As we have seen in Chapter 3, the footings of all walls are very dry, so the actual planting point in the plot that you will have prepared earlier must not be less than a full twelve inches away from the wall – more still if the bed is wide enough – and the clematis must have copious draughts of water, especially in its first season. If there are then any difficulties about protecting the clematis roots with a sunshade plant, a good, thick slab of paving stone placed over them will do.

Planting

Order your plants from a British nursery of repute, preferably one specializing in clematis. The best time for planting is October, but any time up to the end of May is good, providing the ground is not frozen hard or sodden. Even after May is quite permissible, since the plants are always pot-grown.

All being prepared, knock the plant out of its pot carefully, without damaging the frail young stem or dislodging its supporting cane. If the roots are at all dry, put them lightly back into the pot (for convenience) and stand the pot in water for five minutes. Ease the ends of the roots out gently from their spiral coil sufficiently to be able to spread them out. If planting is done in autumn or early winter, cut the stem or stems of the clematis down to a convenient pair of buds about 9 to 12 inches from the ground; don't funk this essential amputation. It should not be necessary in spring planting, however, as the job should have been done in the nursery, but often isn't!

Scoop out a hole of ample size and plant the young clematis so that its root-ball is covered by at least a good inch of soil. Here we deviate from the precepts of Chapter 3, the intent being to defeat the arch-enemy, wilt. The hope is that, if wilt destroys the first shoots, fresh ones will be induced from below the ground, where new roots are likely to have started from the buried nodes.

Then fill in the hole, firm the soil well and water lavishly. While planting keep a watchful eye on the supporting cane, which should be employed to lead the clematis on to its host. This usually means slanting it and it will therefore be profitable to plant the whole ball of soil at the same slant. Try to save the young stem from developing a kink. Finally, as a protection against birds, cats and careless hoemanship, put a cage round the stem of wire netting, twigs, or what you will.

As must be the rule for so many plants, avoid use of the hoe anywhere in the area of the roots, for many of them grow very close to the surface of the soil. And never "fork over" the area where the roots lie.

Servicing

Future care consists mainly in the following measures.

Watering, which I think I have already amply insisted on in these pages.

Tying in and guiding the new shoots where the host is an artificial one.

Mulching. A very important demand of clematis culture. Every spring the root area requires a top dressing of manure, of compost (if reliable) or of peat to which some seaweed or fish fertilizer has been added. Alternatively, an autumn dressing of oak or beech leaves impregnated with a little of the same fertilizer and kept in bounds by some low wire netting, is excellent.

Deadheading, or removing the seed heads after flowering is over. You may feel reluctant to remove the more decorative seed heads, but you should certainly cut them off while the plant is young and not leave them overlong on a mature one; they make very nice embellishments in a vase.

Pruning, which must be a subject apart.

Spraying. Compared to roses and fruit trees, the clematis has few enemies other than the wilt. Powdery mildew will attack some varieties and this can be discouraged by spraying with "Karathane" at the end of June, repeating four weeks later or at need.

Earwigs are a great nuisance in some gardens, nibbling greedily at the leaves and the blossoms alike. The remedy is to spray the plant with DDT or with one of the proprietary concoctions containing BHC. This can be blended into the Karathane spray at need.

Slugs may seriously damage tender young shoots at or just below ground level. A mass of very sharp sand (especially "Cornish Sand") will scratch their bellies and deter them and a proprietary slug killer will account for a few.

Display

In earlier chapters the clematis has been mentioned for its easy adaptability to many uses. The most charming of all, to my eye, is its natural habit of scrambling over shrubs and mounting small trees and sometimes even large ones.

On trees. There are, of course, limitations. No forest giants. No trees of dense, umbrageous foliage. Those of light and airy carriage are to be preferred. The late W. J. Bean, Curator of Kew Gardens, was no doubt right in considering the laburnum ideal for anything but the ultra-vigorous *C. montana.* Other amenable tree-hosts are the rowan or mountain ash, the Judas tree (*Cercis siliquastrum*), the fastigiate cherry 'Amanagowa', the dogwood and crab apple. Old apple, quince and pear trees, due to be pensioned off, are splendid.

Host and guest must be carefully matched; the large-flowered clematis hybrids are quite unsuitable. What we want here are the small-flowered wild species, such as *chrysocoma*, which will reach 30 feet, the much smaller *macropetala*, which would do very nicely for a Judas tree, or *viticella* and its related hybrids (particularly 'Abundance'), which smother themselves in a foam of small flowers in late summer.

Where to plant the clematis in relation to the tree is a very important point that we have discussed in Chapter 3. If the tree is a standard and its upper works are light and airy, as in the laburnum, it will be an advantage if both the tree and the clematis can be planted and grow up together. The viticellas will marry happily at once in this way; *C. chrysocoma* will outpace its host, but can be kept within bounds until the host has built up its limbs. Bear ever in mind that the prime need of the clematis in this situation more than any other is abundant water until it is well established.

On shrubs. These provide us with perhaps the best of all hosts, but they may provide a special problem of their own in new gardens. The host-shrub must be mature, at or near its maximum development. Otherwise, not only will the clematis outgrow it for several years to come, but also the clematis roots and stem will be completely engulfed by the shrub as it pushes outwards year by year. But, given a mature or nearly mature shrub there are few greater splendours in the garden and one may use almost any clematis of restrained growth. In our garden we like very much the pale blue 'Gwynneth' climbing up into the dark green tower of a tall holly. For years we embellished a laurustinus, a shrub that is inclined to be dowdy in the summer, with both a 'Ville de Lyon' and a 'Perle d'Azur', while 'Gipsy Queen' animated, as she still does, the branches of a rather gawky rhododendron.

Some other clematis that do this act most effectively are 'Beauty of Worcester', 'Ernest Markham', 'Mme Edouard André' and 'Comtesse de Bouchard'. Excellent host-shrubs are to be found for them in the witch-hazel, the choisya, *Buddhei alternifolia*, philadelphus, weigela, the barberries and cotoneasters.

Less vigorous clematis, such as *C. alpina* and 'Hagley Hybrid' can be wedded to shrubs of smaller stature, usually keeping to below 6 feet, such as hydrangeas, the Japanese quinces and the shrubby spiraeas. No clematis however (and indeed, no climbers of any sort), should be allowed to spread over shrubs that are grown especially for the beauty of their foliage, such as the dwarf Japanese maple, the gold-splashed elaeagnus and the silver-tinted Siberian dogwood.

Climber on climber. Stunning effects can often be created by a third class of natural host, as I mentioned in Chapter 2, by setting the clematis the congenial task of climbing another climber. Superlative hosts of this sort are wisterias, climbing roses and a pyracantha closely hugging a wall. I would almost go so far as to say that you should never plant a wisteria without planting a clematis also to keep it company.

The same indeed is true of climbing roses, for they keep the happiest company with the clematis, especially those roses that do not flower more or less continuously. There are, I know, people who like to see roses and clematis both flowering together and on the same structure, but personally I prefer to see each alone in its own glory. Thus on the climbing hybrid tea roses, on 'Albertine', 'Elegance', 'François Juranville', 'Allen Chandler' and so on you will plant any of the clematis that bloom after midsummer, including the outsize ones; on 'Mermaid' you would plant an early sort, such as *C. alpina*; but on the ever-blooming 'Golden Showers' and 'Zéphirine Drouhin' you would plant nothing. I say "nothing" but I admit to having had a gorgeous, fuchsia-like mixture in my last garden by marrying the carmine-pink Zéphirine with the small starry blooms of 'Etoile Violette', one of the best of the viticella hybrids.

Walls, fences and pergolas. As will have been abundantly clear from Chapter 2, if not from one's own natural observation, a clematis which is expected to embellish a wall of any sort must be provided with an artificial host (except where it is to climb another climber). I have discussed the various sorts of structures for this purpose in that chapter, but, as far as the clematis is concerned, it is clear that the best of all methods is the plastic-covered chain-link fencing that I described there.

I began to use this some eight years ago not only on walls, but also on fences, lattice-work screens and pergolas. It suits the clematis admirably and, like a certain sparking plug, is a case of "fit and forget". It also comes in very handy as a light and easy way of giving height to a wooden fence. On pergolas, arches and screens the clematis always has some other climber whose limbs it may use, generally the rose, but there are often blank spaces on pergolas, where the soft chain-link mesh will provide an admirable hold for the wandering strands of the clematis.

On all these structures almost any kind of clematis can be grown but they are specially suited to showing off the gauds of the very large-flower sorts, such as 'W. E. Gladstone', 'Mrs Cholmondeley', 'Nelly Moser', 'The President' and so on. The only caveat to be entered is to be sure that the colour of the flower does not clash with that of the wall.

Of a totally different character are the gay golden lamps of *C. tangutica* and the lemon-peel segments of *C. orientalis*, which are arresting in their unexpected forms and colours when grown among climbing roses or on a pergola.

Outbuildings. Few plants are better fitted than the clematis for obscuring eyesores or adorning the commonplace. Here you will usually want one of the rumbustious species, frothing with small flowers, encouraging it to sprawl over the roof as well as draping the sides. *C. montana* and its various delightful colour forms will be too rampant for a small shed and will envelop anything that can give it

40 feet. Usually, the faintly blushing *C. chrysocoma* will be more suitable, or the still smaller *C. viticella* and its offspring, foaming in cascades of deeper purple or vinous red.

Poles. Lacking other means of support, or deliberately creating additional means by which to indulge one's fancy, one may erect tall poles on which to grow the clematis in the open. The height should be not less than 10 feet and a mere bare pole is not enough; it must be one with numerous short branches. These are not always easily procurable and a very good alternative is to encage the pole neatly with wire netting; the netting is bulged 8 inches or so out and round the sides of the pole and nailed or stapled into it all down one side. Another method is to make use of a tall tripod designed for pillar or rambler roses and plant your clematis in the centre of the tripod.

Clematis that look very well on these poles are 'Hagley Hybrid', 'Lasurstern', 'Beauty of Worcester' and, if you can grow it, *C. florida bicolor*, the passion-flower clematis. All these are of moderate vigour.

On north walls. On northerly walls, fences and plantations (but preferably not north-east ones) many clematis are splendid actors, especially if there is some wind-break to modify the buffeting of harsh winds. Of the species, *montana* will not care a hoot whatever the weather and will climb to the top of a fair-sized house if given a host; there are often protective trees on a northerly exposure and *montana* is then just the thing. At lower levels *macropetala* and *alpina* will delightfully embellish a Japanese quince or forsythia growing against the wall or fence or will climb the face of those structures if given an artificial host.

For later in the year you may grow almost any of the easier clematis on a north wall, choosing, for preference, a light blue, pink or white variety. It is in such exposures, rather than in full sun, that such vivid, parti-coloured gauds as 'Barbara Jackman', 'Barbara Dibley' and 'Nelly Moser' show at their best. Here also, late in the season, the lemon-peel flowers of *C. orientalis* will lighten the shadows as with little lamps.

Pruning

In early winter the sere and withered leaves of your clematis and its tangle of twigs look as though scorched by fire and are no advertisement of its delights. You wonder how on earth it is possible for those delights to be re-created out of such frail and seemingly dead matter. The task of pruning, especially with your fingers nipped by the icy air of February, seems a pretty hopeless one and you ask yourself: Where the devil do I begin?

For generations the pruning of clematis has been almost a mistique, wrapped up in a complicated language and very much influenced by the ancestry of each variety. Such methods we must leave to the ardent specialist and we must try to simplify to the largest feasible extent. The actual means of pruning, however, is simplicity itself. You simply cut the stem, with secateurs, immediately above a pair of leaf stalks, within the axils of which there are two buds, which may be dormant or may have begun to shoot.

As on most plants, both the method and the time of pruning depends to a large extent upon whether it flowers on old wood or new wood (Chapter 3). Some clematis flower on the one, some on the other, and some again (awkwardly) on both. As a result, we can make a preliminary simplification by sorting out the varieties into three groups, which are as follows:

Group 1. These are the spring-flowering species and their offspring: *montana, alpina, chrysocoma, macropetala, armandii* (with reservations), etc. These all flower in April or May on wood that has grown the previous summer. Therefore the basic precept is to cut out all the wood that has flowered immediately after it has finished its display. They must on no account be pruned in the winter, the time at which all other clematis are pruned.

What one should aim at is to build up a basic framework during the first two years or so, training the shoots out over whatever area you want to cover. After that the simplest course, after flowering is over, is to clip back with a pair of shears to within about 3 inches of the main framework. This is a simple enough job and quickly done if the plant has been well trained and if you do not leave it too late. New wood will then appear for next year's display; tie this in as necessary. See, however, what is said later about plants grown on trees and bushes.

C. armandii, which is evergreen and not fully hardy, does not care for this all-in treatment; it is best left alone but, if any amputation is necessary, the flowered shoots should be cut back separately.

Group 2. These are the midsummer hybrids flowering in late May or early June; and often again in the early autumn. While the first flowers are forming on side shoots from last year's wood, the new wood is also growing out. This class can give one quite a pruner's headache, for even the doctors of horticulture disagree about it in detail; one will say that, having built up a good framework, you may leave them to look after themselves, but this soon results in disorderly tangles like Neaera's hair or a shaggy bird's-nest. The better but harsher drill is to disentangle all the shoots, tie them in over the widest spread and cut back to some strong pair of buds. Apart from the wearisome disentanglement, this really amounts to just "light pruning". This is done in February, or even earlier; I do it at the end of January in Surrey. Examples: 'Nelly Moser', 'Lasurstern', 'The President' and 'Henryi'.

As for Neaera's mussed-up hair, only the most dedicated lover will have the patience and the hardiness on a February day to sort out the whole horrid tangle. Other gardeners will simply chop them off and await new growth.

Group 3. This is far the easiest. It consists of the hybrids that bloom late in the year on the "new wood" that has grown since the winter. All you have to do is to cut the whole plant down to within 3 feet of the ground or even lower still. This also you do in February (end of January for me). Examples: *jackmanii*, 'Perle d'Azur', 'Hagley Hybrid', 'Gipsy Queen', *tangutica* and *orientalis*.

All groups. Cut all newly planted clematis down to 9 or 12 inches from the ground.

Reflections and Riders. The first lesson that arises from all these divers habits is that clematis, above all plants, should be clearly and durably labelled and that one should keep a little notebook to remind one of the right treatment for each.

A second thought that comes home to one is that the problem is enormously simplified by sticking to one group only, especially Group 3. There are then no complications. Certainly one would miss the charms of the spring-flowering varieties and the gay splendour of those that flower at mid-season, but there is compensation in much else that delights the eye in our gardens at those periods.

A third reflection is that it seems somewhat beyond human patience and dexterity to apply the ordinances of Groups 1 and 2 to clematis that are scrambling over trees and shrubs. Few tasks are more provocative of bad language, especially if the host-shrub is a thorny one, and you feel that the young woman who was required by a jealous goddess to sort out a heap of mixed wheat, barley and oat grains had a much easier job.

I think the answer in this case is not to make the attempt, beyond what is implied by that ambiguous phrase "a little judicious cutting back". After three years or so, when things seem to be getting out of hand and the floral effects are not what they should be, a harsh severance to within about 3 or 4 feet of the ground will clear the air and allow a fresh start.

The two charming spring species *alpina* and *macropetala* will in any circumstances come to no harm by this means for the first few years; after that the secateurs will be hard at work in May, for there will be a lot of dead wood to be removed entirely, as well as the amputation of the shoots that have just finished flowering. *C. montana*, if it gets out of hand on a tree or building, can be lopped off at about 8 feet from the ground in May, or, of course, less hard, provided that the old flowered shoots are also got rid of.

Neglected old plants. These are too often a legacy inherited from non-gardeners or lazy ones of a previous occupation. Here you have two courses open to you. One is to allow them to flower, observing whether they do so in spring, mid-season or later and then prune accordingly. When they have got completely out of hand, with a tangle of dead and rusty wood, they may alternatively be sheared off at about 3 feet from the ground level. Group 2 is here the most awkward to cope with.

A Choice of Clematis Varieties

The following is a limited selection of well-tried and proved clematis species and varieties (or cultivars, if you wish to be in the fashion). I can't claim to have grown them all myself, but, in those instances in which I have not done so, my remarks are based either on observation in other gardens or on the second-hand testimony of two or more specialists of high repute. There are plenty more good ones in addition to those that I have selected, but you are warned that there are also several difficult or "miffy" ones, such as 'Lincoln Star', 'Prinz Hendrik', 'Bee's Jubilee', 'Duchess of Edinburgh' and 'Lady Betty Balfour'.

For readers who might like to start with a ready-made selection of half a dozen, embodying all virtues, I suggest:

jackmanii 'Superba'	'Hagley Hybrid'
'Lasurstern'	'Perle d'Azur'
'Nelly Moser'	'Gipsy Queen'

To these, if more are wanted, might well be added one of the pretty yellow species and one really ought to try to find room for *C. macropetala.*

In the following list, those in italics are species or have specific rank. The group figures in brackets are a guide to pruning.

alpina (Group 1). This species produces masses of nodding, blue, bell-like flowers of the daintiest charm in April and May, reaching normally to about 8 feet. Suitable for any use, but looks best sprawling over a shrub of moderate size. Excellent for a northern aspect.

C. alpina is perhaps exceeded in beauty by some of its special colour forms, of which the best are:

'Columbine.' A lovely, soft, pale blue, with elongated sepals, elegant and graceful; my first choice.

'White Moth.' Small flowers, but fully double, rather like a ballet skirt, and, of course, white. Excellent for a northern exposure or for enlivening any dark corner. May.

armandii (Group 1.) An evergreen and not fully hardy, but good for the warmer counties and for sunny walls elsewhere. If planted in autumn, it should be protected in its first winter as advised in Chapter 3. The leaves are large and leathery in texture and from their axils are thrown out dense clusters of small, creamy-white flowers in April and May. It may grow to 25 feet. The variety 'Apple Blossom' has a faint pink tint and 'Snowdrift' is pure white. The young growth is often brittle and breaks if roughly handled.

Barbara Dibley (Group 2). A gorgeous confection in a blend of petunia red and mauve, with eight long, elegantly pointed sepals. It fades very badly in sun, however, and thus looks best in a northerly exposure or other position of semi-shade. Not a strong grower. May–June.

Barbara Jackman (Group 2). Another large, vivid, barred flower in the style of 'Nelly Moser' and 'Barbara Dibley', in tones of plum-purple and petunia red. The remarks on 'Barbara Dibley' apply. May–June.

Beauty of Worcester (Group 2). A most reliable and attractive clematis with flowers of a deep, rich, Oxford blue, set off by bold, white stamens. At the first flush, coming on the old wood in May, the flowers are double, but a second flush, coming in September, bears single ones. Of moderate vigour.

chrysocoma (Group 1). A vigorous climber up to 20 feet or so, bearing small rounded flowers of white, flushed rose, on extra long stalks in great profusion. The young shoots, leaves and flower stalks are prettily clothed in a silky, pallid gold down. One of the best clematis for climbing trees, clambering over outhouses and enlivening north walls. May, with very often a second crop in the autumn.

Comtesse de Bouchard (Group 3). A reliable and deservedly popular sort, bearing quantities of 5-inch flowers of cyclamen pink of attractively curved habit. A charming consort for 'Perle d'Azur'. July to autumn.

Ernest Markham (Group 3). A fine and showy clematis that will climb to 12 feet, bearing fairly large, broadly overlapping, pointed flowers of a rich, deep carmine, set off by yellow stamens. One of the best. July–September.

Etoile Violette (Group 3). A pretty little hybrid bearing a profusion of star-like flowers in bishop's purple that looks very well among climbing roses. The growth is pretty vigorous. July–September.

florida bicolor (synonym *C. sieboldii*) (Group 2). I include this here not because it is by any means among one's first choice, but because it always attracts the unwary customer's eye at flower shows. Quite unlike any other clematis, it is exceedingly beautiful and, at first glance, looks rather like a passion flower. The flowers are some 4 inches wide with six sepals that open pale green, changing to cream and then white. From this background arises a large, raised, rosette-like boss of petaloid stamens which mature to a bright purple.

To win the heart of this exotic beauty you must give it a warm, sheltered, sunny spot, a rich soil and copious watering. If you can provide those conditions, by all means plant it; if not, don't try. It is not a vigorous variety and a wall, fence or sheltered shrub 6 feet high will satisfy it. June–August.

Gipsy Queen (Group 3). A dusky beauty dressed in rich violet, which is one of the easiest of clematis and most effective when employed to the best use. It needs a light background of cream, pale green or white. I grow it on rambler roses. The flowers measure 5 inches and are produced in rich abundance over a long period from June to the end of August.

Hagley Hybrid (Group 3). One of the loveliest of clematis where one of modest stature is the call. It will grow little more than 7 feet and becomes massed for three months with shell-like, 5-inch blooms of tender cyclamen, embossed with chestnut anthers, flowering madly on new shoots that are produced in rapid succession. The majority of the flowers are carried at eye level. June–September. Excellent on climbing or rambler roses, on small shrubs, on pergolas and arches.

Henryi (Group 2). Large, beautifully formed, white flowers, contrasting with a prominent brown eye, flowering first in May and again in autumn. Beautiful in semi-shade.

Huldine (Group 3). Not one of the easiest, but one of the most beautiful when seen in a favourable light. Having a pearl-white upper surface to the sepal and an under surface of pale mauve which is streaked by a bar of deeper mauve, it has a lustrous, opaline appearance. The colour, however, is not seen unless the flower is illuminated from behind by the sun; otherwise it is white, 'Huldine' must have a position in full sun. July–September.

jackmanii (Group 3). The most famous of all clematis hybrids, bearing 5-inch, rather gappy, purple flowers through July and August. Now surpassed by

***jackmanii* 'Superba',** in which the flowers are violet-purple, with broader sepals. Prolific, vigorous and an everyman's clematis.

Lasurstern (Group 2). This is one of the very tops. The large flowers, which may measure 7 inches at the first flush, have seven or eight undulating, broadly overlapping sepals and their colour, as nearly as I can describe it, is a rich plum-purple – a regal colour of oriental splendour – with stamens of Cornish cream. My own No. 1 clematis. It has a glorious first innings in the period May–June and a second one beginning late in August, when the flowers are not so big. Its modest stature of about 8 feet make it adaptable to many uses and not too severe a headache to prune.

Lord Nevill (Group 2). A very handsome and vigorous clematis with up to eight, broadly overlapping sepals which are crinkled at the margin and coloured a deep, blue-purple, nearing violet. A masculine-looking flower of strong constitution. May–June and again in autumn.

macropetala (Group 1). I have mentioned this species so often that there can be no doubt how warm are my affections for its loveliness.

It never fails to enchant both those newly introduced to it and those to whom it is familiar. It is sometimes aptly called the ballet-skirt clematis, for its gracefully nodding, double flowers are much of that form. The colour is powder blue. The plant may grow to some 12 feet and will charmingly perform any task expected of a clematis. It blooms in April and May, and often gives us a few more in the autumn. Although quite hardy, its beauty is best observed if it is trained along a wall or fence; it will do well in any aspect.

There are three colour forms of *C. macropetala*, of which we may note the following:

'Maidwell Hall.' A very beautiful blue form, which I like the most.

'Markham's Pink.' This is rose-pink, which, to my prejudiced eye is a little out of character.

Mme Edouard André (Group 3). Popular for its easy good nature and its very near approach to true red. The medium-sized flowers, measuring 5 inches, are a vinous crimson, but with a matt finish and cream stamens. In its colour range it is not the equal of 'Ernest Markham' or 'Ville de Lyon' and needs full sun for its best effect. June–August.

Marie Boisselot (or 'Mme le Coultre') (Group 2). An all-white clematis of handsome character, with eight very large, broadly overlapping sepals. A challenge to 'Henryi', which I tend to prefer but which some gardeners find less easy to establish.

Miss Bateman (Group 2). Large, well-formed white flowers with broadly overlapping sepals, enlivened by bright purple stamens. Very attractive. May–June.

montana (Group 1). The virgin's bower or mountain clematis. Enough has been said about this celebrated species to make it clear that it is an exceptionally vigorous one, up to 30 feet certainly and 40 feet perhaps. Excellent for festooning trees, smothering small buildings and so on. Easy, hard as nails, producing great swags of small white flowers in May. The variety *C. m. wilsonii* has larger but skinnier white flowers that delay their appearance until June.

Colour variations on the theme of *C. montana* that are usually preferred to the original, all flowering in May, are:

C. m. rubens. Rather larger flowers of rosy-pink and sweetly scented, with purple tinted leaves.

'Elizabeth.' A beautiful, variation of *rubens* with large, scented, opaline pink flowers, which often, however, do not show their colour until the second season. A little less vigorous than the species.

'Pink Perfection.' A slightly deeper pink; again very good indeed.

'Tetrarose.' Extra large flowers more than 3 inches wide, of rose-mauve with coppery foliage. Of great merit, but the colour is less attractive than those of the other varieties.

Nelly Moser (Group 2). One of the most popular of all clematis, its gaudy splendour attracting the tutored as well as the untutored eye. Vigorous, easy to grow, attaining 10 feet or more without difficulty, it is spangled with large flowers, measuring 6 or 7 inches, which are of soft mauve-pink, streaked with a broad, bold bar of carmine. These dramatic colours bleach badly in full sun and so benefit from partial shade. It blooms twice – in May–June and again in September.

orientalis (Group 3). This is the celebrated "lemon-peel clematis". Its small flowers consist of thick, fleshy, yellow sepals, of nodding habit, opening like the peel of a lemon or pale orange cut into four segments, some 2 inches wide. It is of great vigour, reaching 15 feet, and makes an arresting spectacle. Excellent on a north exposure. You must, however, insist on the form introduced from Tibet by the explorers Ludlow and Sherriff and known as L and S form No. 13342; otherwise you will get something inferior. July to October.

Perle d'Azur (Group 3). One of the most beautiful of all the tender-hued clematis, growing to 10 feet or more and densely draped with 5-inch flowers, which are so near to a true pale blue as to be an entirely suitable favour for all those who cheer for Cambridge. Well known as a charming consort for the pink 'Comtesse de Bouchard'. July–August.

tangutica (Group 3). Another yellow clematis of very distinctive character and delightful form. The flowers are small, less than 2 inches long, but of a bright yellow, formed rather like little Chinese lanterns until they open their four sepals, somewhat in the stance of a snowdrop. Not least of its charms are its spun-silk seed heads, which are to be seen at the same time as the flowers, the early blooms fructifying as the later ones open. The plant has considerable vigour, maybe attaining 15 feet, but its growth is very slender, so that it is seen at its best when rambling at will over another plant. July–October.

There are three varieties or forms of *C. tangutica* that are possibly superior to the species. 'Gravetye' and *obtusiuscula* have flowers of a deeper yellow and Jack Drake's form has much larger ones.

The President (Group 2). A very fine and fairly vigorous clematis whose characteristic is that the flowers do not open flat, but in the form of a shallow saucer. Thus one sees not only the upper surface of purple but also the pallid, silver-barred reverse. Perhaps its special merit, however, is that, in a good summer, it is quite likely to bloom three times – in June, at the end of July and again in autumn.

Ville de Lyon (Group 2 or 3 as you wish). One of the most popular

Vitis coignetiae growing over a garage in Cheshire

Actinidia kolomikta

Above: Cotoneaster wardii; fan-trained

Below: Thunbergia alata, 'Black-eyed Susan'

Lapageria rosea

of clematis and justly so. Also one of the easiest. The flowers, of medium size, are a deep vinous carmine. It will grow to 10 feet or more and is one of the finest scramblers over fairly large shrubs. July to September.

viticella (Group 3). Luxuriant climber to 12 feet or more, becoming smothered with small, nodding, purple blooms of four sepals. Hardly the thing for house walls, but excellent for clambering up small trees. Not liable to wilt. July to September.

There are several varieties and hybrids, of which the following are chosen:

C. v. 'Rubra'. Deep velvety red.

'Abundance.' Soft, vinous purple, with dusky veining; perhaps the best.

'Kermesina.' Wine red.

'Royal Velours.' Rich purple with velvet finish.

Vyvyan Pennell (Group 3). If you like double-flowered clematis, this and 'Beauty of Worcester' are perhaps the best bets. Six inches in diameter, the blossoms of 'Vyvyan Pennell' build up into large rosettes, in the manner of a small dahlia of the "Decorative" class, in a blend of lavender and lilac. Vigorous habit and excellent constitution. May–June.

W. E. Gladstone (Group 3). Enormous flowers, often a full 10 inches wide, are borne on a plant that will grow to 10 or 11 feet. The colour is lavender, with rippled edges to the sepals. A handsome flower, rather too large to ramble over a shrub, but excellent on a pergola or on lusty climbing roses. July to September.

William Kennett (Group 2). A most reliable and easy clematis, if not of distinctive character. Large lavender flowers, with eight, broadly overlapping sepals, are borne on a vigorous plant with tremendous abandon in May and June and again in late summer.

Finally, something out of the ordinary. A close look should be taken at varieties that have been raised with the rather tender ***C. texensis*** as one parent. This species produces flowers of quite different form from those that we have been studying. They are shaped like a pot-bellied urn with a narrow neck and are open-mouthed, somewhat like those tulips that are classed as "lily flowered". The flowers are small, but what is attractive about them is that they are almost scarlet. They flower from July till October.

The result of hybridizing is that we have a handful of varieties with very pretty cherry-red or pink flowers sometimes urn-shaped and sometimes bell-shaped, none of them being larger than 2 inches, except in 'Gravetye Beauty', which is the best and has 3-inch cherry bells. Other charming varieties are 'Countess of Onslow' and 'Duchess of Albany', both in shades of bright pink. Others are 'Etoile Rose' and 'Sir Trevor Lawrence'. A special feature to notice of all these is that they are herbaceous (dying right down to the ground in winter) or semi-herbaceous. They grow to about 10 feet and are good shrub scramblers.

CHAPTER 6

THE CLINGERS

THERE are not many of these. Occasionally they may need a little coaxing, but in the ordinary way they have merely to be planted and away they go on their own. Bear in mind that they are not suitable for tile-hung walls.

Four of them – the Virginia creepers, the ivies, the climbing hydrangeas and the schizophragmas – are very tall, needing a large wall area or a pretty lofty tree for the fulfilment of their destinies.

At the other end of the scale are three of quite modest height – the asteranthera (for those who can grow it), the pileostegia and the easy and adaptable *Euonymus fortunei radicans* – which will suit many purposes in small or large gardens, and are all evergreen to boot.

In between comes the campsis, with its stunning fanfares of red and gold, the only one of the clingers to produce a really dramatic flower display.

The reader will note that, for his benefit, I begin in this chapter to depart from orthodoxy by listing some genera under their more familiar vernacular names.

AMPELOPSIS. See under "Virginia Creepers" and in Chapter 7.

Asteranthera

In *Asteranthera ovata* we have a small, uncommon climber which is evergreen and fairly hardy but not easy to please in the drier counties. A good plant for small gardens that have the right conditions, it is unlikely to go more than 15 feet and is freely hung about at mid-summer with small, slender trumpets of a rich red, carried on slender limbs that are clothed with small, dark green, roundish leaves.

In its native Chile the asteranthera inhabits damp, mossy woodland and is a natural tree climber. In our gardens, therefore, we must give it a moist soil, a shady situation and a reasonably mild climate. It is excellent for ground cover and, if planted in a damp, woodland situation, will, like ivy, creep along the surface and then clamber up any tree it encounters. Or we may save it the trouble of creeping and give it at once a chance either to climb up a small, spent tree, over which it will spread an evergreen shroud, or to ascend a shady northerly wall (no other). An acid soil is to be preferred.

Campsis

Also known as *Bignonia* and *Tecoma*, this genus provides us with the most gorgeous of the clinging plants, growing to some 30 feet or more and, in a good season, breaking out into a splendour of clustered trumpets in shades of red and orange. This earns it the fancy names of "trumpet vine" and "trumpet creeper".

Most of the campsis seem to be pretty hardy when established, but they expect a genial summer and are not likely to flower well unless given a south or west wall, or a large pergola in full sun. Their frailty is that, if subjected to alternating hot days and cold nights at flowering-time, which is late August and September, their buds drop off without opening. If planted in the autumn, they must be protected for their first winter in the manner described in Chapter 3. Once they have got their toes well in, they make fast growth. They are deciduous.

The campsis flowers on new wood grown in the current season. Accordingly, the method of pruning is to cut these shoots hard back to two buds from their junction with the parent stem in late winter.

The best known and hardiest species is:

C. radicans, which produces very fine clusters of challenging, deep orange trumpets with great freedom from among its decorative, pinnate leaves, which resemble those of the wisteria in miniature. It develops a thick, woody trunk, also like the wisteria. Old plants sometimes partially lose their grip on their host and have to be supported.

More dramatically beautiful, however, is the hybrid:

Madame Galen, a magnificent plant in which the trumpets are of a rich, deep salmon-red. It is a cross between *radicans* and *grandiflora*,

FIG. 9. *Campsis radicans*, showing its holdfast roots.

but can't be expected to do itself justice unless given a very hot summer.

For those fortunate enough to live in the warmer counties an even finer campsis is:

C. grandiflora (or *chinensis*), a superb plant that bears clusters of a dozen or more trumpets that are deep orange and red, wider mouthed than is *radicans*. It is less hardy than the other two and must have a hot wall. It is also less able to cling than the others and needs a few ties to retain company with its host.

Euonymus

The botanists have recently changed the name of a most useful, decorative and easy species of euonymus long familiar to us as *E. radicans*. We are now expected to call it *E. fortunei* var. *radicans*.

Small brother of our native spindle tree and of the sombre Japanese hedger, it is evergreen, very hardy, of restrained height but spreading broadly. Its leaves are small, neat and dense. If planted near a vertical structure, most of its branches begin almost at once to lean towards it and to develop clinging holdfast roots. Thus it is a first-rate plant for a small area of wall or fence or for clambering over a tree stump. It will nicely fill the wall space beneath a window, will succeed in apparently any kind of soil, in full sun or in shade and is not so insistent on a liberal water supply as most others.

Most people rightly prefer *E. fortunei* in one of its coloured forms, particularly the handsome silver-leafed forms, in which the dark olive green is broadly margined in platinum. This may be found in catalogues under diverse names such as 'Variegatus', or 'Silver Queen' or 'Gracilis', a charming form with tints of pink and purple as well as silver. To the initiate gardener the general visual effect of all these is of a dwarf, variegated ivy.

There are also the varieties 'Colorata', which turns a showy purple-red in winter, and 'Minima', having minute leaves and adaptable to climbing over rocks.

I don't recall having seen the silver-leafed *E. fortunei* growing much more than about 12 feet high, though it is reputed to go higher. On reaching maturity after several years, it begins, like the ivy, to lose its holdfast roots and becomes stiffly shrub-like, but this propensity can be defeated by clipping it when it shows signs of reaching this stage, so that it continues to behave in an attractively juvenile manner. When planted in open ground, its "aerial" roots become real roots, so that it spreads widely.

HEDERA. See under Ivy.

Hydrangea

In early chapters I have mentioned *H. petiolaris*, one of the climbing hydrangeas. This is the best of them, although deciduous. It will climb by its holdfast roots to the tops of lofty trees or cling to the face of a very large wall. It is very hardy and entirely suitable clothing for a north wall.

Unfortunately *H. petiolaris* sometimes sulks at the foot of its host before making up its mind to start climbing but it then does so very quickly. Furthermore, it is not fitted for bearing flower until it is some years old, because they are not borne on the main clinging stems but on outgrowths that develop later.

When it does flower, in June, it produces trusses some 8 inches wide of the same floral style as the "lace cap" hydrangeas. These differ from the mop-headed hydrangeas in having a slightly domed, nearly flat, formation (or "corymb"), in which a multitude of very small florets is encircled by large, showy but sterile ones. In *H. petiolaris* these florets are white.

Two other climbing hydrangeas ought to be mentioned:

H. anomala has smaller and more rounded corymbs, with glossy new foliage, but is less hardy.

H. integerrima is evergreen but has little floral interest. Its inconspicuous flowers are arranged in columnar panicles and it is not an adept climber.

Compare *H. petiolaris* with *Schizophragma*, in this chapter.

Ivy

(*Hedera*)

Ivy, they say, is coming back into fashion, like fuchsia and pelargoniums. It deserves to do so, like some other good Victorian things

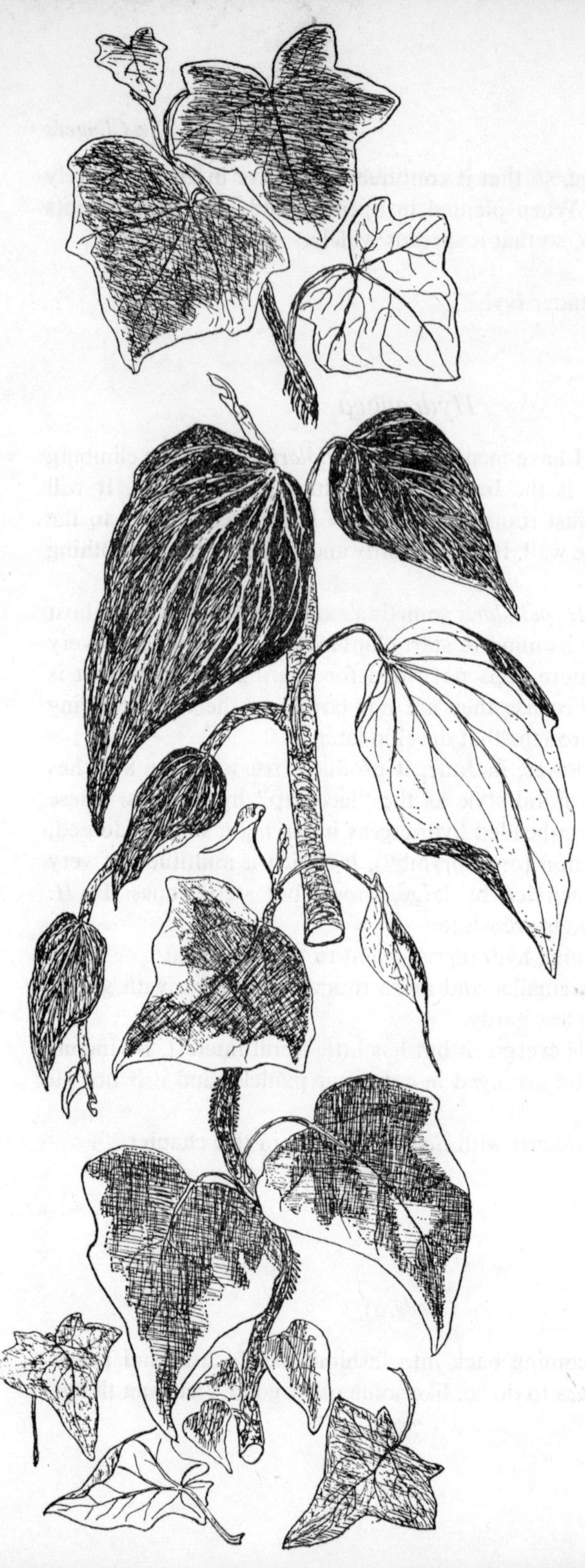

FIG. 10. A gallery of ivies. At top, *Hedera helix aureomarginata*, followed by *H. colchica*, *H. canariensis* and, at foot, three leaves of *H. sagittifolia*.

that now seem to be forgotten. It has beautiful leaf form, often beautiful colourings, is evergreen, is adaptable to many uses and (with rare exceptions) bone-hardy.

In Canada and the United States (they tell me) our common English ivy, *Hedera helix,* is much prized. Beautiful species come from other lands also. Both our own and the strangers have swept into favour in the "house plant" cult and it is to be noted that nearly all of them are hardy outdoors.

There is little evidence that ivy does any damage to well-built house walls. It cannot root into the fabric, its real roots being below ground. Indeed, by shedding off the rain, it keeps the wall dry, though it may, to be sure, harbour spiders and sparrows. Thus it is a good insulator for houses with a particularly bleak exposure. Similarly ivy does no harm to trees when it climbs them, unless it reaches to the very top. But it does take air and light away and the form and grace of good specimen trees are certainly upset. There are, of course, many uses for ivy besides the clothing of walls or of trees that are of little value. They are excellent for masking outhouses and they are the best of all ground-cover plants in woodland. They can be charmingly employed in the Victorian fashion as edgings to flower beds. They are particularly handsome for screening purposes, a purpose that we might study a little.

Several years ago I concocted the wood "fedge". Whether I was the first to do so is unlikely, but certainly the word has stuck. By a fedge I meant an old wooden fence overgrown on both sides with ivy, giving it the appearance of a hedge. Not only does it look extremely well, but also the ivy will long outlast its wooden host; and it will be the ivy that holds up the fence, not the other way round. It need hardly be said that this dodge is far cheaper than building a new fence, which nowadays costs the earth. One needs a plant at about every six or eight foot spacing, according to how impatient one is.

Where a screen is desired and no fence exists, a fedge can be specially devised. For a low screen, a split chestnut fence can be run up for the ivy. A taller screen can be made from stout posts of any height that is practicable, loosely filled in with lattice work or trellis.

We have seen that *Euonymus fortunei* stops putting out its clinging pads when it reaches maturity and begins to behave as a shrub. Ivy does the same, and it is likely to do so before long if stopped from climbing by man. When grown on a house, it should always be stopped at about a foot short of the eaves, after which it will begin to throw out flowering shoots, bearing very small blossoms, followed by bunches of black berries, which are models of design. When the ivy shows signs of fulfilling this natural function it should be restrained by clipping it back.

Let us now pick out some of the best of the various ivies that are at our disposal for these uses.

The Canary Ivy. Of this noble, large-leaves species from the Canary Islands there is a superlative variety often called 'Gloire de Marengo' (*H. canariensis* 'Variegata'), in which the shield-like leaves are blended of olive-green, silvery-grey and white, with here and there a flash of pink. It grows very fast and makes a wonderful picture against a red-brick wall or anywhere else where it may be employed, its colours often being more brilliant in winter than in summer. It is reputed to be not quite hardy, but in many gardens in the south of England at any rate has withstood the worst of winters, though the young leading shoots have occasionally been nipped by very hard frosts. If there is doubt, it had better have a sheltered aspect.

The Persian Ivy (*H. colchica*). Entirely hardy, this is a very handsome species, ranking second only to the Canary Ivy. Its large, polished, leathery leaves, ovate in form, are often 9 inches long. The favoured variety of this species is *H. colchica* 'Dentato-variegata', in which the leaves, curiously diverse in size, are of a soft green conspicuously margined or splashed with yellow and sometimes entirely yellow – a very fine ivy for all and every use.

The English or **Common Ivy** (*H. helix*). This celebrated species, much famed in song and fable, has sported into innumerable varieties in shape, size, colour and habit. Their nomenclature, as so often in sports from the wild, is very confusing, various aliases being bandied about, and what may be 'Minima' in one nursery may be 'Congesta' in another. The only safe thing to do, if one is particular, is to go to a good nursery and pick one's choice; unfortunately, however, few nurseries nowadays have a large assortment to choose from. What most attracts the fancy is any gold or silver variegation and there are several available. To name a few:

'Buttercup' (also known as 'Russell's Gold' and 'Golden Cloud') is probably the best of the golden shades.

'Tricolor' (alias 'Elegantissima' and 'Marginata Rubra') is a beautiful ivy with small grey-green leaves margined with white and with a deep pink edge in winter.

'Jubilee' (or 'Jubilee Goldheart') is a fine and lively sort, with the gold in the centre and green bands around.

'Silver Queen' (alias 'Argentea Elegans' and 'Marginata') has broad cream borders and pink tints in winter.

'Glacier' (a favourite with growers of "house plants") has small neat leaves of pewter grey, edged and flecked with white – a delightful little ivy.

'Aureo-variegata' (also known as 'Chrysophylla' and 'Angularis Aurea') is a tempting variety in the nursery with its irregular splashes and suffusions of yellow, but it has a strong tendency to revert to green.

Other varieties of *Hedera helix* offer us very attractive variations in leaf form, apart from colour. Of such are the arrow-headed 'Sagittaefolia', the slender 'Pedata' (like the print of a bird's foot) and the shield-like 'Deltoides'.

The Irish Ivy (*Hedera hibernica*). This has large, bright green leaves, with usually five triangular lobes, and is too coarse for ornamental uses but is often employed for utilitarian ones such as ground cover.

PARTHENOCISSUS. See "Virginia Creepers".

Pileostegia

The little-known *P. viburnoides* is one of the very few evergreen clingers of modest growth. Its "ceiling" is 20 feet and on the rare occasions when it is seen it is usually much less. It has slender, leathery leaves rather like those of the rhododendron, from which it throws out abundant quantities of irregular panicles densely crowded with wee flowers of pale cream in August and September.

Close relative of the hydrangea, the pileostegia is quite hardy and is suited to any good, loamy soil and in any aspect. Not highly distinguished, but very pretty when in flower, useful for many purposes and no trouble.

Schizophragma

This high climber is so closely related to the climbing hydrangea that very often it is difficult to distinguish the two apart until near inspection or until the flowers bloom. The deciduous foliage is very similar and the flowers, like those of its relative, expand into the nearly flat clusters of the "lace cap" hydrangeas. The difference lies in the fact that, whereas the sterile, showy, outer florets of the hydrangea have four or five sepals, those of the schizophragma have only one, but very large and more conspicuous though undistinguished in colour. These, with their inner mass of very small florets, appear in July.

Like all the hydrangeas, the schizophragmas expect a fairly rich soil and plenty to drink. They can be put to exactly the same uses, but flower most freely in the sun. The two species to notice are:

S. hydrangeoides is clothed in toothed foliage very like that of the hydrangea and its flower clusters are ringed with the conspicuous single sepals described, which are pale cream, heart-shaped and anything up to 1½ inches long.

S. integrifolia. In this favoured species the sepals are relatively enormous – more than 3 inches long – drooping and fluttering like so many dolls' handkerchiefs and putting up a much better show than its sister. Its name comes from its foliage, which is untoothed, broad and rounded but coming to a long, fine point.

Virginia Creepers

(*Parthenocissus*)

The appalling muddle in the matter of names created for us by botanists, nurserymen and others speaking with many tongues is my justification for this unorthodox heading. Those included here were sorted out by the botanists some years ago from the genera *Vitis* (the vine) and *Ampelopsis* (vine-like) and given the apt and charming name of *Parthenocissus*, which means "virgin ivy".

Unfortunately, very few nurserymen have yet taken to this name, so that these most handsome of all clingers are found under diverse

FIG. 11. Some vine leaves and a "virgin ivy". At top, *Vitis coignetiae*, followed by *V. vinifera* "Brandt" and *Parthenocissus henryana*.

names, which confuse and deter the ordinary gardener, who is not safe even if he asks simply for a "Virginia creeper".

The parthenocissus are climbers of powerful physique and long reach, remarkable for the beauty of their vine-like leaves, which, in the borrowed vision of Andrew Marvell, "transpire at every pore with instant fires" when they become ensanguined with dazzling red or crimson hues before they fall in autumn. In particularly favourable conditions they will also produce small bunches of grapes.

Not all have self-clinging pads, but those selected here do, though they may need a little artificial support at first.

The virgin ivies are usually employed for the adornment of large walls, but are far more dramatic clambering up a tall tree, when in autumn they seem to resemble an enormous torch. The late V. Sackville-West spoke of the beauty of a Virginia creeper climbing among the white and black arms of a silver birch, its branches festooned with great swags of scarlet and looking like a stained-glass window. Scarcely less dramatic is their employment as a canopy for mutilated oaks, sycamore and other parkland trees that are to be found overshadowing the garden of many small town and suburban houses built in rows on the land of some large estate that has been cut up by a speculative builder. Selections:

P. quinquefolia. This is the true and original Virginia creeper, found in that state in the days of the Pilgrim Fathers. It is identified by its five-lobed leaves, which are rather matt green in summer and rich crimson in autumn. Very fine and not quite so powerful a climber as the next, but in some opinions, not quite so good. Most likely to be found in catalogues as *Vitis quinquefolia.*

P. tricuspidata. A magnificent Asian creeper, therefore not Virginian. Here lies the danger of ordering a "Virginia creeper", for you may get the American instead of the Asian. Oddly, in America it is known as the "Boston ivy". The leaves of this parthenocissus are very diverse in shape, either broadly egg-shaped or having three leaflets, and in autumn they become incarnadined a dazzling fuchsia-crimson. The plant will grow 60 feet high. Aliases: *Vitis inconstans* and *Ampelopsis veitchii,* both names being still freely used by nurserymen.

P. henryana. To my mind this is the most beautiful of all the "virgin ivies", having a refined character and charming colourings, the veins being picked out in silver and pink on the three- or five-fingered lobes. It exhibits its artistry, however, only in the shade, which means a northerly wall or one of some other aspect in which direct sun is kept off by trees. In the autumn the leaves colour superbly. Its only faults are that it is a slow starter and that its tiny suction pads dislike very rough surfaces. A twiggy pea stick helps to get it going. Nearly always found in catalogues as *Vitis henryana.*

P. thomsonii. Another "virgin ivy" of fine colourings, very close to *henryana.* In spring the young growths are claret and in autumn the whole plant is crimson.

See also *Ampelopsis*, next chapter.

TECOMA. See Campsis.

CHAPTER 7

THE TWINERS

THIS chapter includes a wide diversity of plants that climb either by coiling their tendrils or leaf stalks round their host, in the manner of pea, clematis and many others, or by twining their stems round their supports and often round their own limbs, as in the wisteria. Nearly all are very suitable for growing on walls, pergolas, trees or shrubs and lattice screens, or for forming reposeful arbours. If designed to climb walls or fences they will need an artificial host of the sort described in Chapter 2, but most of them can be allowed to ramble haphazard over walls and roofs of sheds, after a little initial fixing.

In general, the stem-twiners or "twisters" are well suited to climbing trees but are best not used on shrubs of any value, because of their tendency to strangle their host. The tendril climbers, however, are quite safe on shrubs, except for the vines, which will smother them too much. The clematis is the shrub climber *par excellence*, but in Gulf Stream counties the mutisia and bignonia may well take its place. I remind the reader also of the excellent value to be gained from setting the tendril climbers to climb another climber or a wall shrub.

A "short list" for selectors would be composed of:

the wisteria,
the honeysuckle,
the celastrus,
the lapageria where conditions permit,
the passion flower,
one or other of the ornamental vines
and, of course, the clematis.

Close runners-up to these are some less well known twiners, especially the schizandra, the actinidias, the jasmine-like, evergreen trachelospermum and the mandevilla. Several plants have their special uses, such as the splendid *Vitis coignetiae*, the parti-coloured

A tender honeysuckle, *Lonicera sempervirens*

The 'early Dutch' honeysuckle, *Lonicera periclymenum belgica*

Actinidia kolomikta and the scented, evergreen holboellia. Yet others may appeal for one reason or another and anyone fortunate enough to have the right conditions for *Tropaeolum speciosum* is mad not to grow them by the dozen.

It is amusing to note how the stem-twiners vary in their methods of twisting. Thus *Wisteria sinensis*, the akebia and the celastrus twine clockwise, whereas *Wisteria floribunda* and honeysuckle (like the scarlet runner bean) go anti-clockwise. The hand of man is helpless to change these instincts, so that, in trying to guide a shoot in a particular direction, it should be wound in its natural spiral.

Those that are marked with the symbol § are fitted only for the Gulf Stream counties or for sheltered places inland, so that impatient readers who live elsewhere may if they wish pass them by.

Actinidia

This is a very interesting tribe that we do not see very often in this country. Yet its members are hardy, very ornamental and easy to grow in any good, fertile soil. They are entirely suitable to growing on walls of one sort or another or to form an arbour, and some will twine their way up into any tree of moderate size which is of no particular interest. Some produce gooseberry-flavoured fruits which are eaten in Japan and China and which are occasionally seen here in the more expensive fruit shops.

Only two actinidias, however, are normally grown in this country and, apart from being both deciduous, they are of completely different characters.

A. chinensis. This aristocratic species is known aptly enough colloquially as the "Chinese gooseberry". It is a robust, fast-growing twiner, reaching to maybe 30 feet, and has an amusingly shaggy appearance. Except for the flowers, all its parts are hairy – the shoots, leaves and fruit – the hair on the shoots being positively red.

The leaves are up to eight inches, large, broad and plentiful, so that it makes a good shade-plant to train round an arbour, as you might a vine. It gets away very quickly as soon as spring breathes warmly and grows very fast, twisting its furry tip eagerly upwards.

The flowers of the Chinese gooseberry appear early in August in small clusters. They are of cream, deepening to buff, pleasant enough

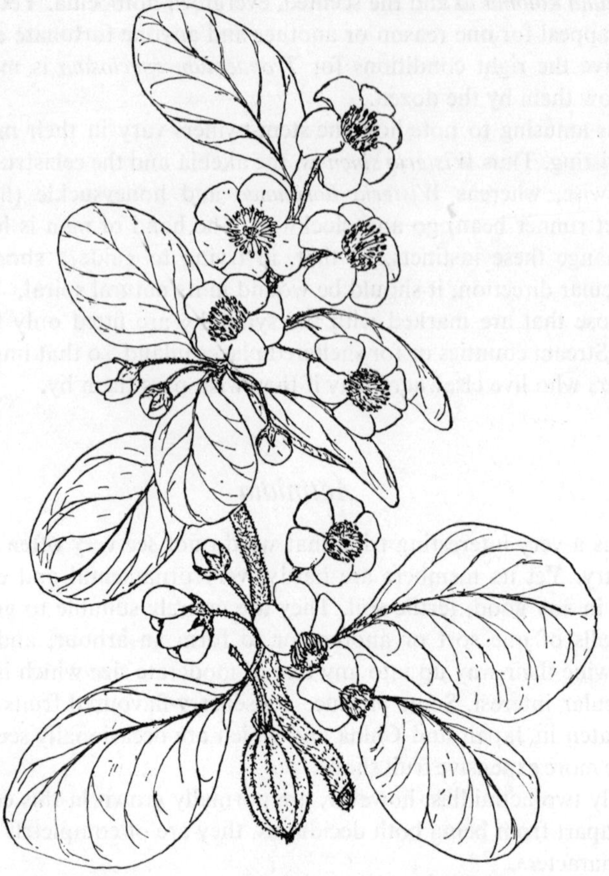

FIG. 12. *Actinidia chinensis* in blossom; a small fruit is shown separately at foot.

and sweetly scented but exciting no rapture. Many of them are unisexual, but some are bisexual, so there is hope for some of the amusing fruits if August is hot. They are like plump sausages up to two inches long, covered in brown hair. The flesh has a mild gooseberry flavour. In New Zealand and elsewhere selected forms are grown commercially for their fruit, which is then of superior quality.

A. kolomikta. This is very pretty and totally different from the Chinese gooseberry (though it does sometimes have its own little fruits). A slender and elegant beauty, rarely growing more than 10 feet high, it is cultivated entirely for the charm of its coloured foliage. The heart-shaped leaves, about 5 inches long, start green, after which they may become streaked with white and finally, in whole or in part, turn pink or pearly white. This delightful tri-colour effect, however, seems to be displayed at its best only on a warm south or west wall and it may also be affected by soil conditions.

Thus this actinidia is essentially a plant for some sort of wall, where it will pay its caretaker to train the stems out decoratively. The very small flowers are white and unisexual and it is the male plants that contrive the more handsome colour displays.

For some reason *A. kolomikta* is very attractive to cats, and young plants had therefore better be protected against them.

Akebia

This is the genus celebrated for its handsome violet or plum "sausages", but they are rarely produced. A good, hot summer and probably hand-pollination are needed for them to fructify.

The akebias are stem-twiners of moderate vigour, more suitable, I think, for scrambling over old trees or clothing outbuildings than for other purposes. For the walls of the main house there are better plants, though the five-leaved species is certainly decorative. They are evergreen in the warmer counties, deciduous or semi-deciduous in others, and are quite hardy, growing fast. They are not of much value in a northerly aspect and, obviously, if you want the fruit, they must have plenty of sun.

The small flowers of the akebias, which have sepals but not petals, are interesting and soberly attractive, though of no great beauty. Arranged in little, drooping racemes, they are in various tones of purple, composed mainly of innumerable, minute, male florets, watched over, as it were, by two much larger females, like a couple of nannies escorting a crowd of infants. The sausage fruits that may result split open to reveal a number of black seeds embedded in white pulp.

Only two akebias are generally cultivated in Britain:

A. quinata is the better of the two. As its specific name implies, it is characterized by its five-foliate leaves, which are deep green and neatly formed. In the little hanging trusses of flowers which appear in April, the males are pale violet and the females purple-brown. The sausages, about 3 inches long, are really more like ducks' eggs, if you can imagine a plum-coloured duck's egg with the bloom of a fresh plum on it.

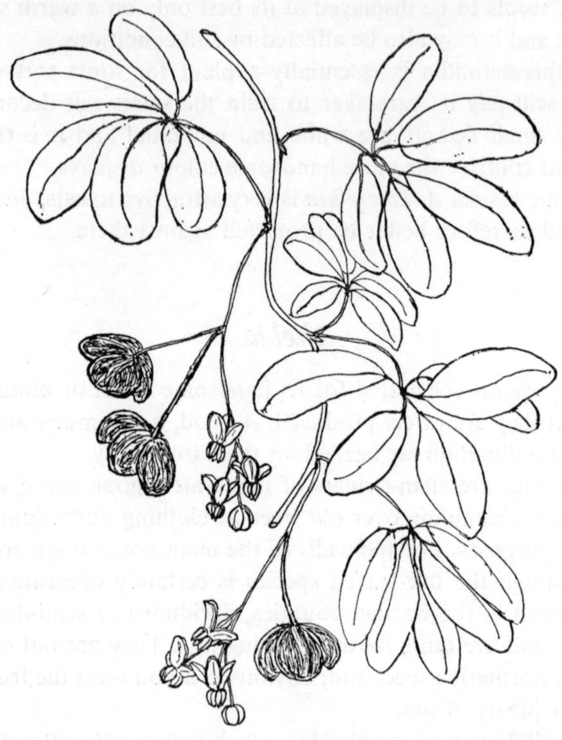

FIG. 13. *Akebia quinata,* the larger flowers being the females.

A. trifoliata (or *lobata*). This obviously has its leaflet in threes. The female florets are an inky-purple, and the sausages, which may be as long as 5 inches, are pale violet.

Ampelopsis

This is a tribe in the kingdom of the vines to which the botanists have granted independence. It is still often listed under the style of *Vitis*, the tree vine, to which it has a close resemblance in the twining tendrils by which it mounts its host, unlike the other main tribe in this kingdom, the Virginia creeper, which climbs by clinging.

The chosen one of this tribe is *A. heterophylla*,[1] a luxuriant climber, whose leaves are very variable in their shapes, as the name suggests. It fulfils much the same sort of purposes as the Virginia creeper on a smaller scale, growing to 20 feet or so, and if planted on a hot wall will produce pretty bunches of small, turquoise grapes. There is a particularly engaging form of it in which the leaves are splashed and tinted with pink and white, not nearly so strong-growing and better fitted for small places; this is usually known as 'Elegans', but may also be 'Variegata' or 'Tricolor'.

More unusual is a very attractive species with fern-like foliage and orange berries on slender stems, which will handsomely clothe a large arch or pergola as well as a wall; this is *A. aconitifolia*.

Aristolochia

A rather over-rated genus that gets publicity in gardening columns from its not very appropriate nickname of "Dutchman's Pipe", through a fancied floral resemblance to the drooping, china-bowled pipes smoked in some parts of the Netherlands (but much more so in Germany).

Most aristolochias are hothouse plants and not very choice ones at that. Some are non-climbers, some stink and many take a long time to flower. The only species that deserves our notice is:

Aristolochia durior. This is the so-called Dutchman's pipe, the flower being a bent tube which, as Mr Jackman rightly points out, is really more like a saxophone than a Dutch pipe; but then, our ancestors who gave it its nickname were spared the acquaintance of that musical instrument. Appearing in June, they are very small – little more than an inch long – largely obscured by the foliage and not beautiful, though amusing enough. The main part of the little tube is greenish-yellow and the upturned mouth maroon.

In fact, the foliage is much more attractive than the flower, being composed of large, heart-shaped, pale green leaves up to 10 inches

[1] Now monstrously re-named *A. brevipedunculata* var. *maximowiczii*, but a name that will be shunned by all but the most dedicated botanists.

long, quite suitable for quickly clothing an arbour. The plant is deciduous and not trustworthy for hardiness in the colder areas.

Bignonia

The bignonias of my youth have been cruelly treated by the botanists and nearly all have been banished to the tents of other tribes. Thus *B. radicans*, the best of the hardy species, has been carried off to those of the *Campsis* (see Chapter 6).

A few, however, have refused to obey the official edict and continue to be known as bignonias by the world at large. One of these is *B. capreolata*, which has resisted the professional ruling that it should be re-styled Doxantha. It also hangs on confidently to its American vernacular name of "cross vine", which takes its origin from the fact that, when the stem is cut transversely, a cross appears.

The cross vine is not so much grown now in this country as formerly, though it is very handsome, with clusters of orange, funnel-form flowers, 2 inches long, from the leaf axils, in June.

It climbs by tendrils growing from the tips of the leaves and is said to be capable of reaching 30 feet in this country. It grows handsomely at Radlett, Hertfordshire, but is not generally to be advised where there is not a warm south wall.

A good loamy soil is needed.

A variety *atrosanguinea* has purple flowers.

For *Bignonia venusta*, see Chapter 10.

Billardiera

A pretty little climber, useful to gardeners interested in unusual plants, but hardy only in the warmest counties. The only one to be attempted outdoors is the Tasmanian *B. longiflora*. It twines by very slender stems to about 5 feet only, is clothed with small, evergreen leaves and in July bears small, solitary, yellow, rather tubular flowers; in September, if the climate is to their liking, these develop into handsome indigo-blue, almond-shaped berries, which are edible. Good on a trellis.

FIG. 14. *Celastrus orbiculatus*, in flower and in fruit.

Celastrus

Here we have a race of an unique character, providing us with our finest climbers for late autumn and early winter. In summer they are rather dull plants and their splendour lies in their copiously borne fruits, which are small but brilliant and displayed on elegant, branching sprays. They are scarcely larger than a pea, but when ripe in November they turn orange and the fleshy outer seed coat (or "aril") splits into three portions to disclose the red seed within, in the same manner as the seeds of our native spindle tree (*Euonymus europaeus*), to which the celastrus is related. Their small flowers are of no account.

Known in America as "bittersweets", the celastruses are stem-twiners, are wholly self-supporting once attached to their hosts and are often employed as tree-scramblers, which is their habit in nature. Several are hothouse plants, but those for our money are hardy, deciduous and easy to grow in any decent soil. The favoured species is:

C. orbiculatus (synonym: *C. articulatus*). This will scramble up to about 30 feet, writhing and corkscrewing over its host and itself in a dense tangle and being showered with gold and scarlet fruits in big, beaded swags from late September onwards and often throughout the winter. It will flourish in any aspect and in any reasonable soil and is beautiful for cutting. The caveat to be entered is that all plants are not reliably bisexual and therefore a hermaphrodite form must be positively demanded from the nurseryman.

A few other species are also commercially available, including *C. hypoleuca*, with large, handsome leaves that are pale blue on their under surface.

CLEMATIS. See Chapter 5.

CROSS VINE. See *Bignonia caprelata.*

DOXANTHA. See *Bignonia capreolata.*

FLAME NASTURTIUM. See Tropaeolum, later in this chapter.

Holboellia

Handsome, evergreen, sweetly scented stem-twiners of lusty growth with polished, dark-green, leathery leaves having three or more lobes. The flowers are small, inconspicuous and unisexual, but males and females are carried on the same plant, and the important thing is their wonderful scent, which is borne afar. If planted on a wall, pergola or trellis the laterals ought to be spurred back to get maximum flower.

H. coriacea is quite hardy, growing to 25 feet or more, with trifoliate leaves. The male flowers are purple and the females a pallid green, produced in April and May.

H. latifolia has three or more lobes to the leaf and the colours of the male and female flowers are the reverse of those of *coriacea.* The purple fruits, if produced, are edible. Sometimes listed as *Stauntonia latifolia* and at its best only in the milder counties.

Honeysuckle

(*Lonicera*)

Iconoclasts of one sort or another are always trying to destroy one's most cherished beliefs. Recently some verbal vandal tried to persuade

Lonicera tragophylla

The Passion-flower, *Passiflora caerulea*

Abutilon milleri

Abutilon vitifolium album

Corokia cotoneaster

Sophora tetraptera

us that the "woodbine" of Shakespeare, Milton and others of our traditional poets, was not honeysuckle but something else. This "something else" it no doubt has been in very early times and in the United States, but not here in Britain. Quite certainly Oberon's "lush woodbine" that "quite over-canopied" the bank on which the nodding violets grew was the common honeysuckle.[1]

The word "honeysuckle" is also of extremely ancient usage, being apparently first applied to the clover and other honey-bearing plants, and Bacon, contemporaneously with Shakespeare, used the word in both senses when he described the "Honey-Suckles (both the Woodbine and the Trifoile)". Thus "woodbine" seems to be of more ancient application than "honeysuckle" to the genus *Lonicera*, and Bacon is a witness that perhaps the Elizabethan era marks approximately the date of transition when "honeysuckle" began to mean particularly the woodbine. To Milton, a little later, it is still "the well-attired woodbine".

However, these are all matters for the boffins of etymology and, whether honeysuckle or woodbine, we may concern ourselves only with the growing of our dearly-loved wanderer of the woods and hedgerows. And we may note at the outset that its natural habits dictate, in part at least, the conditions that we must provide for its well-being.

These conditions are, primarily, shade, a very moist soil, an annual mulch of leaves and a host by which it may rise into the light – very much the same conditions, indeed, as the clematis loves, but perhaps with rather more emphasis on a shady and moist root-run. Honeysuckles are never really happy when planted in full sun or in dry soils and are unhappiest of all when expected to grow on a hot wall. Indeed, to display themselves to their full pitch of grace and bearing on any wall requires some attention, skill and discernment on the part of the gardener. The most promising aspect is a north-west one.

Honeysuckles are essentially scramblers over other shrubs and trees, though in gardens, as I have already mentioned, they should not be used on shrubs of any value, because of the strangling effect of their twining stems. Perhaps their most charming use of all is to give coverage to the framework of an arbour, which they will "over-canopy" in the fashion that enchanted Oberon. They are also

[1] The passage in *Midsummer Night* IV, i conflicts and has been much discussed by learned commentators.

delightful in their cottage habits of climbing over arches and gateways and sprawling over sheds. More unusually, they look splendid on tall tripods or branched poles among low shrubs or herbaceous plants. But, however employed, they must be given a cool, shady and moist root-run.

These precepts, it is true, apply with less force in the cooler counties and in those having plenty of rain; and it is to be noted that ample water, whether natural or man-provided, is a good corrective for a soil that is otherwise too hot. Moreover, the few evergreen species stand the sun better than the deciduous ones.

Pruning is not often necessary when honeysuckles are grown in a natural manner, but on walls or over small arches some restraint is necessary. This is best done by shortening the flowered side shoots by about half their length.

Honeysuckles are often a prey to greenfly, especially when in full sun. The pest can readily be foiled by spraying the plant with a systemic insecticide, such as Murphy's of that name or Abol X.

Of the 180 species of honeysuckle, most are non-climbers, with which we are not here concerned, and there are only a dozen or so climbers that have any interest for the gardener. Their flowers are of tubular form, but on some species are widely expanded at the mouth, trumpet-wise, with bold projecting stamens. Nearly all are of pallid hue in their early phases but deepen to stronger ones as they develop. In the cussedness of nature, those that have the sweet breath which we expect from a honeysuckle are florally the least gorgeous, yet pretty enough in their muted tints.

In accordance with our general practice of segregation for the purpose of convenience, let us look first at those species and varieties that will be wanted by the gardener whose first demand is for scent.

SCENTED HONEYSUCKLES

L. periclymenum. This is the original woodbine of our hedgerows and coppices, but there are two varieties that are superior to the wilding for garden purposes. They are very popular and very easy, but give their more splendid displays only when given their natural conditions. The two varieties are:

The "Early Dutch" honeysuckle (*L. p. belgica*), with flowers of rather pale rose-purple on the outside of the tubes and the lips yellow within, beginning its mission in early May.

The "Late Dutch" (*L. p. serotina*), with similar flowers of slightly deeper hue, beginning in late June or early July.

Both of these flower a second time, so that, between them they provide charmingly scented blossom for nearly six months. They will climb to 20 feet if given the chance.

L. americana (or *L. grata* or *L. italica*). This fine honeysuckle is a hybrid between the European *caprifolium* and the Italian *etrusca*, so the reason for its American name is not outwardly apparent. It forms elegant and charming sprays about a foot long, crowded with flowers both at the tip and in the leaf axils. The flower begins white, deepens to yellow and becomes flushed with rose. It flowers from late June until early August and may in the best conditions climb anything up to 30 feet high, providing a spectacular display.

L. japonica This is an evergreen honeysuckle of no great beauty but with a scent of oriental opulence. It grows very fast and lustily, with slender, downy shoots, and is one of the best plants for screening outbuildings or for draping an arbour, where one may recline under its swooning scent if one is not smothered by its foliage. Two varieties of it are more often grown than the species itself. One is *L. j. halleana*, with more downy shoots and with flowers of pale biscuit in axillary pairs, by no means spectacular but borne continuously through the summer from June onwards. The other is *aureo-variegata*, which is pretty stingy with its flower but is grown for the golden network on the light green leaves, which many consider attractive.

These evergreen orientals are often grown over tall trellis work to make screens, when they should be planted 8 feet apart. They develop into dense tangles, like "Neaera's hair", with all the growth on top, but they can be kept in nice balance by pruning hard back every spring, ideally to the base of last season's growth if you have the patience. They are a bit drab in winter.

All the above are hardy and are the most widely grown of the scented species. Three other scented species are much to be recommended in the warmer counties or for inland gardens with warm corners. They are:

L. etrusca. An Italian honeysuckle of which the finest form is the variety *superba*, in which the flowers, arranged in groups of three on the numerous side branches, begin yellow and finish orange. Growing fast and energetically to 20 feet and more, it thrusts out purple young shoots that grow several feet in a year when happy. Its fault is that it does not flower when young, but after that amply makes up for its youthful slackness.

L. heckrottii is only a half-hearted climber, but is useful for covering an old tree stump or the like. The colourful flowers are yellow and mauve and make a fine show for three months from June onwards.

L. hildebrandiana §. This is the "Giant Honeysuckle", a magnificent species, no doubt, for anyone lucky enough to have the right conditions for its success, but I have never seen it except in one of the greenhouses at Kew. It is probably useless to attempt growing it anywhere outside the Gulf Stream gardens. In such cushioned environments it appears to have scarcely less vigour than the Virginia creepers, but is shy to flower unless given a hot wall. It is an evergreen, with large, tough leaves and large trumpets up to 6 inches long, beginning off-white and colouring to orange. Bean records that the finest specimen he saw was growing on a wall in Colonel Stephenson Clarke's garden in the Isle of Wight.

DISPLAY HONEYSUCKLES

Here we leave the scented species, all inclined to be a bit pallid, and turn to those that have more gorgeous wardrobes, but no sweet breath. The way to treat these creatures, I suggest, is to plant them a little beyond reach of one's nose, so that all who pass by may admire and not be disappointed. For the honeysuckle is, to most people, like a rose; first you look, then you sniff and you always feel a bit let down if there is no aroma. Of the following species, the first three specially command attention.

L. brownii. This is the "scarlet trumpet honeysuckle", a vernacular name that sufficiently describes its brilliant colour. There is (or was) a fine specimen at Sissinghurst Castle in Kent. It is a hybrid from two North American species, quite hardy and not too rampant. The flowers are rather small, but abundantly borne when the plant is happy and it makes two displays between May and August. A splendid honeysuckle for smaller gardens.

There are several varieties of *L. brownii*, all pretty much the same, but possible 'Fuchsioides' is to be preferred.

L. tellmanniana. Another splendid hybrid and of considerable vigour. The flowers are borne in clusters of from eight to twelve, rose in the bud, opening to wide-mouthed trumpets, 2 inches long, of a rich, warm deep-hued gold, flourishing in June and July. It seems to make its finest display where its roots and lower members may enjoy considerable shade, indeed, often complete shade.

L. tragophylla. Visually, this is undoubtedly the most sumptuous and dramatic of all the hardy honeysuckles. Large, opulent trusses of a bright and brilliant gold are displayed with handsome maroon, stem-clasping leaves on a plant that may grow 20 feet high. The blossoms are slender but wide-mouthed trumpets fully 3 inches long, with the stamens projecting eagerly, and there may be anything up to twenty such trumpets in each truss. Like *L. tellmanniana*, this species is most successful when its roots are in moist soil and almost complete shade.

L. sempervirens. The magnificent, evergreen "trumpet honeysuckle" of the United States, is arrayed in splendid clusters of orange and scarlet, but is not hardy enough for the colder counties, though it does well in such climates as those of the London and Oxford areas.

L. henryi. This species is sometimes offered. Its very small, red-and-yellow tubes are not much catch, and what value it has lies in its glossy, evergreen foliage, which forms a good screen for an extent of up to 30 feet.

Lapageria rosea

This is one of the greater glories of our gardens, conformable to the cottage plot as to the lord's demesne wherever the right conditions exist.

A genus with only one species, the lapageria is an evergreen stem-twiner with slender, wiry shoots, which grow to an average height of about 15 feet but which can easily be persuaded to keep a lower level if required.

Its flowers are bell-like or lily-like or trumpet-like, as you will, but slenderly so, the mouth not widely flared or reflexed. They are about 3 inches long and dangle from the wiry stems in threes, twos or sometimes singly on richly laden, sculptural swags. They have six segments, of a waxen, glossy texture and of a warm, glowing, rose-crimson. They adorn the plant in late summer and early autumn, flowering first on the old wood and then on the new wood of the summer's growth, and are accompanied by leathery leaves that are roughly heart-shaped, coming to a fine point. Though it may seem odd that a climbing plant should belong to the lily family, its relationship is clear when the long, slender buds appear and open their shining fleshy segments to one's gaze.

Perhaps it is not surprising that such a sumptuous creation should be exacting in its needs. It is not wholly tender and will resist a little frost, but is not tough enough for the colder counties. It must have plenty of warmth in summer, but, in what might seem a contradiction, wants a shady situation, as might be provided by a north-west wall. Moreover, at its roots it expects an acid soil and abundant supplies of water during summer and a damp atmosphere is particularly to its liking.

All these dictates point to our western and south-western shores as being the most promising for the lapageria's fulfilment, but in fact it is to be found in favoured places inland also: wherever there is a warm, sheltered nook in partial shade with a lime-free soil that is naturally moist (but well drained) or kept moist by the hand of the gardener in summer. Anyone who can provide these conditions is mad not to grow as many lapagerias as there is room for. Whatever site is chosen it should be one in which the luminous, dangling bells are displayed to the best advantage. They are well suited by the plastic-covered chain-mesh of which I have spoken or by ordinary wooden trellis.

Two special points in cultivation of the lapageria are to take the utmost precaution from the beginning against slugs, which are its deadly enemies, and to remove with care all dead stems, which restrict its freedom of flowering.

Where the outdoor conditions do not exist the lapageria can quite easily be grown in relatively small greenhouses in which a little warmth, shade and the right soil can be provided. In more spacious days they were often (and still occasionally are) trained over the corridors between greenhouses, where, if you were imaginative, you might suppose that they were ringing a peal of welcome as you passed beneath.

There is a beautiful white variety and other variations, not easily come by.

LONICERA. See Honeysuckle.

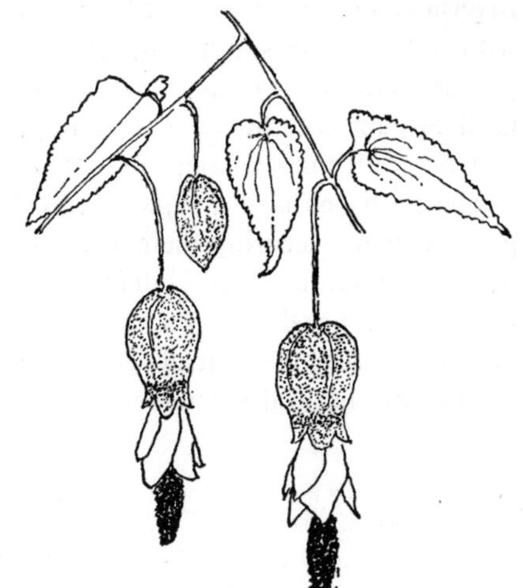

FIG. 15.
Abutilon megapotamicum.
See page 118.

Mandevilla

A beautiful, slender, stem-twining, sweetly scented, deciduous plant that is sometimes called the Chilean jasmine. It certainly has a floral resemblance to the jasmine, though none botanically. I speak of *M. suaveolens* (or *M. laxa*), a refined, elegant, slender shrub, hardy enough for southern England on sun-bathed walls or fences or trained over arches in a warm corner. There are fine specimens in Oxford and Essex, not the warmest of localities.

The ivory-white flowers are tubular with widely flanged mouths and are displayed in clusters of six to eight blossoms for two months or so from June onwards, followed by remarkably long, thin seed pods. They are set off by long pointed leaves. Everything about the plant is slender and relaxed. A milky sap flows from the young shoots if they are cut. Twelve feet is about the limit of growth. A favourite greenhouse climber.

Another good species is *M. tweediana*, very similar to *suaveolens* but not easily obtainable.

Mutisia §

Another beautiful race that has an undeserved reputation for tenderness, for it confounds expectation by flourishing in Edinburgh and

Inverness and other seemingly unpromising climates when provided with a protective south wall. It may often be seen in south coast gardens, but one is bound to regard the mutisias as mainly plants for Gulf Stream counties and their happiest hunting ground seems to be Cornwall; but see under *M. oligodon.*

The mutisias have a highly individual character. They are evergreen twiners, securing their hold by pea-like tendrils from the tips of their leaves and are embellished with large, elegant, daisyform flowers composed of gay and sometimes gaudy ray florets, arching boldly out from the central yellow disc.

They are natural scramblers over other plants, with a sprawling,

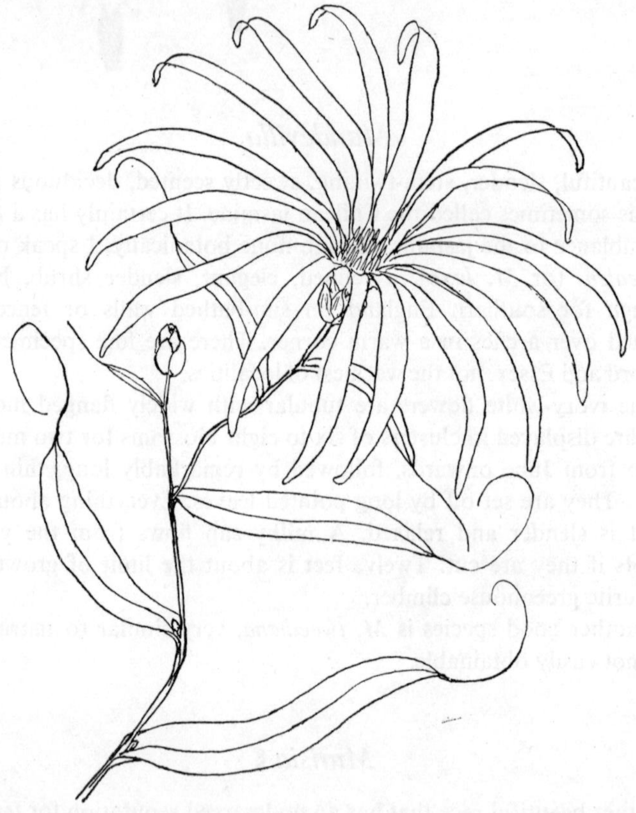

FIG. 16. *Mutisia decurrens.*

untidy habit, and are happy if planted in the open under some deciduous shrub and allowed to wander over it at will. But they are adaptable to walls, particularly if provided with some other wall shrub as a host, in the manner described for clematis. They are not, as a rule, wildly rampant and are thus within the compass of a small garden and they have a phenomenally long flowering season.

The mutisias appear to succeed in a diversity of soils, though

FIG. 17. *Mutisia oligodon.*

Bean prescribes "a perfectly drained, light, sandy soil". What is of critical importance, however, is that, like the clematis and the honeysuckle, their feet and lower limbs should be in shade, moist shade, untouched by the sun. They further enjoy a generous covering of stones over their root area. They should be planted in spring and protected against their deadly enemy, the slug.

In Britain many mutisias expect to be coddled in greenhouses, but the following is a selection of those that can be expected to succeed outdoors in the appropriate conditions; elsewhere they can be grown in greenhouses with just enough heat to keep out the frost. Opinions differ on the relative hardiness of the various species.

M. clematis has large and showy daisies of a brilliant orange-scarlet, suggestive of a gerbera, protruding from an elongated neck wrapped in scales. They are on show from May and all through the summer. Of vigorous habit, the plant may reach 20 feet or more, with very nice pinnate foliage.

M. decurrens. Huge flowers, up to 5 inches wide, with ray florets of deep orange, like an outsize marigold with arched petals, are borne from June to August on a plant some 12 feet high. Not always an easy customer to please, but the best known. Where really happy, it may reach to the top of a house on a sunny wall.

M. ilicifolia. Relatively hardy and known as the "holly-leaved mutisia", its specific name being derived from its dark green, leathery, spiny foliage. The flowers are about 3 inches wide, the ten or twelve ray florets being coloured a lilac-pink and almost stalkless. It blooms continuously the whole summer. Height, about 12 feet.

M. oligodon. A far smaller plant and inclined to be prostrate rather than climbing, but with beautiful satiny pink flowers and small leaves rather like those of the holly-leaved mutisia. Quite hardy in Surrey and Sussex; frozen solid in a pot at Ascot in the record freeze of 1963 and quite unharmed.

M. retusa. Of fairly recent introduction, this species may perhaps prove to be the hardiest, as self-sown seedlings have been freely produced in the celebrated garden at Nymans, in Sussex. The flowers are a tender pink and carried on long stalks. About 15 feet.

Passion-flower

(*Passiflora*)

Some 300 species of *Passiflora* exist but I think that we ought to confine ourselves to one only – the beautiful, exotic, curiously wrought and tantalizing blue Passion-flower, which is *P. caerulea.*

Few plants give more delight in the delicacy and ingenuity of their construction and in the legendary associations attributed to them. Few are so apparently unpredictable in their behaviour until the underlying reasons are discerned. Of all the problems sent in by anxious gardeners, few are more frequent than the question: why doesn't my Passion-flower bloom?

Nearly all "the books" tell us that it must be grown on a warm south wall, yet the late Vee Sackville-West reported instances of its flourishing and even regularly developing large crops of its fruit on a cold, easterly one in the gardens of two cottages in mid-Kent, which is not a warm locality. One is told that it is not hardy, and certainly a hard frost may cut it to the ground; yet new shoots spring up readily from the crown.

Thus the Passion-flower has clearly not to be labelled as a Gulf Stream plant and little is needed beyond some patience to enjoy its delicately chiselled blooms. The form so excited the early missionaries in its native South America that they saw in it a living symbol of Christ's Passion.

To them the circlet of innumerable, thread-like purple filaments, which supply most of the colour to the blossoms, represented the crown of thorns. The protruding round-tipped stigmas of the female organ were the nails with which Christ was fastened to the cross. The five prominent anthers of the male organ were the five wounds. The five sepals and five petals, milky white and lying close together to form the background to the whole exquisite design, were the apostles, barring Judas Iscariot and Peter, the cock-crow waverer.

How do we produce this emblem of such tender associations? Let us concede at once that, despite the Kentish examples and others of which I know, the Passion-flower does like warmth in summer and prefers Cornwall and Devon to Norfolk or Aberdeen and a south wall to a north one; beyond that one cannot dogmatize. It also expects abundant water. In Cornwall, where it gets both warmth and water, it freely produces its orange, egg-shaped fruits as a bonus to its summer display.

Otherwise, the first (and unexpected) necessity is a rather poor, stony soil. In rich soils it is apt to run all to leaf, with few flowers. Where the soil is naturally rich, it can be devitalized by mixing in plenty of stones (thus preserving moisture) and its root-run ought certainly to be confined, in the manner used for figs, by sinking a wall of bricks or corrugated iron or the like, about 18 inches deep, restricting its liberty to about one square yard. Some of the most productive that I have seen were growing in limy soil, but I think that the Passion-flower is really indifferent.

Even given these conditions, however, we must make up our minds to the fact that the Passion-flower will occasionally not bloom until it is two or three years old; it will then do so over a long period from June to September. After that, some simple pruning should be exercised in winter in order to step up production and to prevent a smother of top-heavy growth.

This means: (*a*) cutting back the strongest shoots by one-third or more of their length and (*b*) cutting the stronger side shoots back to about four buds. This you do about the end of February. Don't touch the short, twiggy shoots, as it is on these that the flowers are borne. Thus the guiding light is to encourage as many of these short, twiggy side-growth as possible.

Climbing as they do by curling, pea-like tendrils growing from their leaf axils, the Passion-flower, when planted against a wall, likes very much the plastic chain-link fencing that I have described. It also looks very charming when climbing over another wall plant such as a close-clipped pyracantha, but you must then naturally be a little careful about clipping the one and pruning the other.

In addition to the usual purple-blue of *Passiflora caerulea*, there is a variety named 'Constance Elliott', a beautiful connoisseur's piece finely chiselled in ivory. There is a famous one at the celebrated garden of Sheffield Park, in Sussex.

PERIPLOCA. See Silk Vine.

Polygonum

Everyone must know this express-speed climber foaming in creamy, tumbling waves like an agitated sea breaking on a rocky reef. It is grown alike in cottage, suburban villa and country mansion gardens, often in inappropriate places and much too cribbed for space. It is horribly named by the botanist *Polygonum baldschuanicum*, after its remote place of origin in Turkistan. Its nickname of "Russian vine" is more convenient but scarcely appropriate.

As hard as nails, the polygonum is a deciduous twiner, wreathing knots round any convenient host and round itself. Its shoots will leap up to 15 feet in a season, growing almost visibly, and will ultimately attain a reach of some 40 feet. It will do very nicely for smothering a large outhouse, but it undoubtedly puts up its best show on an old tree, where its display from July to October is quite sensational, smothering the host in a froth of large, loose panicles in which the cream can be seen to be faintly tinted with pink. After flowering it leaves behind a tangled mass of light brown shoots.

If the plant at any time gets too big for its boots, it will cheerfully endure being cut back as hard as you like.

Schizandra

Most schizandras are of little floral interest, but the red species is very handsome and showy, though its flowers are small.

This is *S. rubriflora*, sometimes called *S. grandiflora rubriflora.* It may grow to 15 feet, with slender, ruddy, intertwining shoots and pendulous, rather globular flowers of deep crimson in April and May, looking like large cherries before the petals and sepals (which are exactly alike) expand fully.

One should try to site this schizandra where the hanging flowers will stand out like little lamps, trained out on a long screen or over a large arch or summerhouse, but it does very well on a wall and prospers on a north one, for it dislikes too much direct sun. It seems to prefer an acid soil.

A few other schizandras are sometimes grown, but their flowers are very small. Indeed, their fruits, which are a brilliant red in grape-like clusters, are more handsome than the flowers, but all the species are uni-sexual, so that the female will not bear unless consorted with a male. *S. chinensis*, however, is very pretty with its small rose-pink flowers.

Silk Vine

(*Periploca graeca*)

The silk vine has been cultivated in Britain since early Stuart times and is quite hardy, but is seldom seen nowadays, for the curiously muted hues of its flowers do not appeal to everyone.

These flowers, an inch wide, are green-flushed-lemon on the outside of the petals and maroon within. The lobes of the petals open out at the tips, rather star-like, and are covered with silky hairs, being displayed in loose, long-stalked clusters in July and August. The silken hairs are again prominent when the flowers are followed by their long, pencil-slim fruits, which, when ripe, split open to reveal a quantity of seeds each of which is tufted with long silky whiskers.

The silk vine is a deciduous stem-twiner, with narrow, polished, dark green foliage. The stems and leaves exude a milky sap if cut. It grows to 20 feet or more and will do in any reasonably good soil. For those who want to grow it, perhaps its best use is on an old unwanted tree, unless a pergola or large arch or trellis can be spared. It is not well suited to walls, and in any case it should be planted well beyond reach of one's nose, for its odour is atrocious and it could just as well be called the "stink vine".

Other species of *Periploca* are occasionally cultivated.

Stauntonia §

A vigorous, stem-twining evergreen, akin to *Holboellia* (q.v.) hardy in the south-west. The species grown is *S. hexaphylla*, in which the very small flowers are white, tinted violet, some male, some female, and sweetly scented. The foliage is leathery and polished, as in *Holboellia.*

Trachelospermum

Beautiful, lustrous, evergreen stem-twiners, with scented, jasmine-like flowers, hardy enough for all but the colder counties but more successful in the warmer ones. They display themselves best on walls, which they will cover with an ivy-like profusion of glossy foliage, and in all but the milder climates prefer a warm southerly or westerly one, though they will tolerate some shade. No doubt they would be equally well suited to a sunny arbour, where their sweet scent and their charming clusters of small flowers could be enjoyed in July and August. The stems and leaves exude a milky sap.

The chief species obtainable are:

T. asiaticum. This is probably the hardiest. The small leaves provide a close and dense coverage up to some 15 feet, crowded in July in clusters of small cream and buff florets, but less richly scented than the next species.

T. jasminoides. A stronger plant with larger leaves, but reported to be less hardy than *asiaticum*, yet the most beautiful of all. The flowers resemble those of white jasmine and breathe a rich, swooning odour. Few flowers give one a sweeter welcome. There is a variegated version in which the leaves are margined and splashed with ivory and often become flushed with crimson in winter. The same flushing may be seen in the bronze-leaved variety *wilsonii*, which is not always a willing trier.

T. majus. Yet more lusty than *jasminoides*, able to cover a whole house, and rather more hardy. The flowers are again white and the leaves sometimes colour up vividly.

Tropaeolum

All the "nasturtiums" of popular speech are properly tropaeolums, the true nasturtium being the watercress,[1] and in the "flame nasturtium" we have the most gorgeous of the breed and one of the few that is actually less often called by its popular name than by its legal one, which is *Tropaeolum speciosum.*

Anyone who for the first time beholds the sheeted splendour of this gay stranger from Chile is at once halted in his tracks and filled with envious desire. Its vivid scarlet mass of "nasturtium" flowers not only impress the vision but also seem to speak of blazing suns and tropical languor. But in the latter regard it is deceptive and, as a whole, its needs are very special.

These needs are: an acid, leaf-mould soil, ample rain, shade, a cool, moist situation and an annual dressing of decayed leaves, or good, well-rotted compost or old manure. Thus it takes most kindly to our western seaboard and probably its happiest hunting ground is the west coast of Scotland. The finest specimen I have seen was in Galloway, where, on the north wall of a house, it threw a scarlet cloak over its host, which was, as I remember, a climbing hydrangea.

It is true that fine examples are sometimes to be seen in the south, but, on the whole, it is unlikely to reward the gardener in the eastern

[1] *Rorippa nasturtium-aquaticum.*

and home counties, and particularly in the London area. A moist atmosphere is important. But, wherever it is attempted, a shady northern aspect is the thing, either climbing on another wall plant or else rambling over shrubs in the shade. It looks marvellous on a holly.

Strictly speaking, the flame nasturtium is a trifle out of place in this chapter, as it is not equipped with the same manner of climbing mechanisms as the others. It is a rambler and a herbaceous perennial, dying down to the ground every winter except in the very mildest districts. It has rather fleshy, tuberous roots, which should be planted in a *horizontal position*.

Vines

(*Vitis*)

Any of the Bacchanalian vines that are cultivated specially for wine or desert can, subject to their hardiness, perfectly well be grown on walls or fences, thus providing the gardener with two dividends. These are the "fruiting vines", varieties of *Vitis vinifera*, the "common grape vine". Two very good ones are 'Royal Muscadine', a *chasselas* type of small green grape so often seen in French shops, and 'Muscatel'.

What we are concerned with here, however, are the "ornamental vines" some of which are themselves varieties of *V. vinifera*. A few of the other ornamental vines do produce edible fruit of sorts, but what we look for is splendour of foliage and there are plenty of these for us to choose from.

Until fairly recent years the genus included several tribes that had close associations with the true vine, such as the Virginia creepers, and the ampelopsis. These have all been granted their independence and we are now left with a smaller race of which, for our purposes, the chief characteristic is that they all, with rare exceptions that we can ignore, climb and clamber by means of curling and twisting tendrils. This they do in nature, of course, by wandering over other shrubs or up trees. By encouraging our garden vines to imitate nature's practice, wherever there is a tree or a shrub of little value, we can achieve some stunning effects, particularly with the superb purple-leaved vines that are noticed below.

Crinodendron hookerianum

The primrose jasmine, *Jasminum primulinum*

Jasminum polyanthum

Solanum crispum

Itea ilicifolia

More formally, but in a fashion no less picturesque, we can use them to drape around and above arbours where shade and seclusion in the heat of the day are the purpose mainly desired, so that the mind may, like Andrew Marvell's, "withdraw into its happiness". With a suitable framework, they will climb up the sides and over the top, forming solid walls and ceilings, through which none can peer and nothing penetrate except the rain. If the framework is of "rustic" timbers and very open, the shoots will need to be tied in and they will also need to be tied horizontally when required to form a ceiling.

This is an old, old way of growing vines, whether ornamental or fruiting. So also is the pergola, where you are again inevitably reminded of Marvell's "luscious clusters of the vine" dangling down into your mouth.

More practically, but still by no means prosaically, the vines perform a splendid service where a screen is desired to blank off some object or some vista, but it will not, of course, be evergreen. Fences, trellises, outhouses, are quickly covered and, of course, walls are entirely suitable and they may be of any aspect.

The vines of our desiring have eager appetites and do best on a diet of rich loam, fortified with manure. They are content with lime, or without it. If planted in autumn, behead the cane at about 3 feet 6 inches and do so without fail before the end of December, for the sap begins to rise soon afterwards and vines bleed if cut in this state. The result of the execution will be the production of several new shoots which will grow with great speed and vigour and which can be trained out in any manner you wish – espaliered, fanned or grown at random.

When grown in the restricted forms required for arbours, pergolas and so on the shoots should be lightly pruned once or twice in summer and cut hard back nearly to their main stems before the end of December.

We will leave the varieties of *Vitis vinifera* till the last and look first at some other species that will most repay us. Among these *V. coignetiae* stands out as the lord of them all wherever there is space for its strapping physique; but gardeners in small places will find a study of *V. flexuosa parvifolia* profitable.

V. amurensis. A fine, lusty vine, with strength enough to climb quite a big tree. The very large, lobed leaves are green in summer, turning in September to richly varied tones of rose, ruby or purple.

V. coignetiae. This is the grandmaster of them all wherever there is room for its powerful limbs. It is unsurpassed in the practice of mounting a tall tree, into the heights of which it will clamber 60 feet or more, creating a magnificent spectacle. Its enormous leaves are often eight inches wide when mature and sometimes more. They are beautifully wrinkled and in autumn are charged with rich cornelian and rose topaz, obligingly hanging on for several weeks in their full splendour of colour and accompanied by little bunches of dark purple grapes.

Alternatively, *V. coignetiae* will do very well covering the walls and roof of a large shed, providing there is some means of support. It should certainly not be attempted where space is limited.

V. davidii (synonym: *V. armata*). Another splendid vine of rich autumn colouring, its leaves being nearly as large as those of *coignetiae*. Its sign-manual, as its synonym tells us, is that the young shoots are armed with numerous thorny bristles.

V. flexuosa parvifolia (synonym: *V. f. wilsonii*). Quite different in character from the large and masculine vines that we have just noticed, this is a small and dainty variety, with slender stems and leaves only 2 or 3 inches long. Its elegance is enriched by a lustrous, metallic sheen of bronze-green glistening on the upper surface of leaf, which, when young, is purple beneath. A beautiful little vine for small places.

V. labrusca. Not to be compared with the preceeding species for splendour of autumn foliage, but extra hardy and useful and bearing small grapes, with a musky or "foxy" flavour, which a few people appear to find edible.

V. pulchra. A vigorous sort with gleaming leaves that turn blood-red in autumn. Also known as *V. flexuosa major,* which gives an idea of its character.

V. thunbergii. Of moderate vigour, with bold leaves that bear a rust-coloured felt beneath and that become rich crimson in autumn.

We now come to the ornamental varieties of ***Vitis vinifera,*** from which two or three varieties of exceptional merit are here chosen.

'Purpurea.' The finest of the lot, I should say. The leaves come a handsome claret and later turn purple. Known as the "dyer's grape". To gardeners with an eye to fine colour groupings this offers what the celebrated Browne would have called "great capabilities", particularly with such grey-leaved plants as *Senecio laxifolius* and the silver varieties of *Senecio cineraria.*

'Brandt.' Here the leaves do not colour till autumn, when they assume stunning hues of crimson, orange and pink. The dark purple grapes are edible and make excellent vinegar, much better than the common tarragon.[1]

'Apiifolia.' This is the "parsley vine", with finely shredded leaves; very attractive.

'Incana' is the "dusty miller" vine, with leaves covered with a down that looks like cobwebs.

Wisteria

This is the noblest climber of all. Given the chance, the wisteria will soar 80 feet into the heavens, challenging the hues of heaven itself with its magnificent mantle in blended tones of azure, lilac and mallow. Equally well it will, when old enough, cover a horizontal spread of 200 feet along a garden wall or along the balustraded terrace of a mansion. On a small house it can be led round to embrace all four walls in its arms. On a tall one it can be led outwards and upwards between windows in the manner of a toasting fork to surmount the fourth storey in a waterfall of blues.

This recital of its prowess serves not only to demonstrate its vitality but also to warn anyone who is tempted to plant it in too confined a space. The wisteria can indeed be imprisoned in a fairly small cage, but it requires some skill and a good deal of attention to do so. Its great strength and its fleetness of foot may impel it to commit wanton damage unless carefully supervised. It will crack open drainpipes by thrusting between them and the wall. It will insinuate itself under tiles and heave them up; it is particularly fond of doing so on tile-hung walls and one that I inherited on my own tile-hung house had regretfully to be sentenced to death after a five-year struggle.

Indeed, one must face the fact that, unless allowed to wander at will up a big tree or over a large outhouse, the wisteria demands a good deal of attention from its master. Probably nine out of ten that one sees have been allowed to become tortuously coiled round themselves like so many intertwined snakes, for the wisteria will twine round its own limbs with as tight an embrace as it will round

[1] Crush the fruit in a wooden tub, leave it for a fortnight to ferment, then strain off the juice into bottles. Stopper the bottles with a twist of cloth or paper, not with corks.

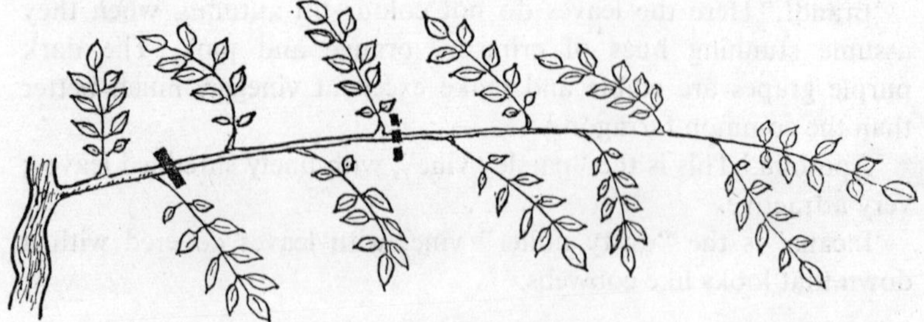

FIG. 18. Pruning a wisteria. Summer-prune at the broken line, winter-prune at the thick black one.

any other object. Bushy outgrowths are also suffered to develop, spoiling the plant's display and limiting the production of its blossoms.

The first rule, therefore, is to train out the shoots of the plant in the directions that you dictate while it is still young and to build up a permanent framework. You must be master of it from the beginning, just as you must be on the fruiting vine, the treatment of which is very similar. Afterwards, as also on the vine, you must perform at least two pruning operations, one in August and one in winter, both simple enough.

For the summer pruning, you shorten the new, leafy shoots to about the fifth compound leaf, which will be approximately a foot from its junction with the parent stem (see Fig. 18). Then in winter you cut the shoot right back to two buds (they are very obvious) and it is from these that you will get next year's benison of flowers. Personally, I do the summer pruning in stages and begin nipping back the young shoots early in July with finger and thumb, a little at a time – a process, however, which becomes tiresome when the plant is big.

That is about all there is to wisteria culture. You must give it a reasonably good soil, but not necessarily a rich one and you had better plant it on a warm wall, wherever its far-reaching arms may subsequently go. Unlike the majority of natural climbers, it is very happy with its roots in full sun.

Neglected old plants inherited from a previous owner can be cut hard back without fear to some new starting point convenient for its orderly redeployment, for the wisteria can put up with any amount of rough handling and always comes up smiling with undiminished spirit.

I have spoken so far mainly about walls, in particular reference to house walls, but the wisteria is equally well suited to being trained along the beams of a pergola or a long screen of rustic or lattice work, where it looks very handsome indeed and is easily got at for pruning and for the tying-in that will be necessary. Indeed, it is less trouble when given such assignments than when set to climb a house wall, which will mean frequent use of a ladder. With a great deal of patience and a little skill, wisterias can also be grown as standard trees.

Furthermore, though the spectacle is rarely seen in this country, the wisteria is a sensational tree climber and will think nothing of getting to the top of a good-sized oak. It should be allowed to do so, however, only on trees that have passed their prime or that have been ruined by some ignorant tree lopper.

People who have visited Lord Iveagh's garden in Surrey will remember the very long and lofty pergola hung with all sorts of species and varieties of wisteria. They are of great and special interest but they serve to show that there is nothing to beat the most familiar and rightly the sovereign choice of all – ***Wisteria sinensis***. It flowers in May with big, grape-like clusters (racemes) of scented pea-flowers that are approximately blue and usually it presents us with another but smaller crop in August from the current year's shoots. There is a white form, *alba*, and a double-flowered form.

Other species of wisteria that deserve notice are:

W. floribunda macrobotrys. This is remarkable for producing enormously long racemes of flowers – over 3 or 4 feet long in this country and even larger in its native Japan. My own experience, however, has been that it produces jolly few of them in making this mighty effort and that it takes a long time to think about it. This variety was long known under the easier name of *multijuga*.

Other varieties of *W. floribunda*, which are no larger than sinensis, are the white 'Alba', the indifferent pink 'Rosea' and 'Violacea Plena', which explains itself. Florally, the significant difference between this Japanese species and the familiar Chinese one is that the flowers of *sinensis* all open simultaneously on their clusters, whereas those of *floribunda* open successively from the base. The Japanese is also far less vigorous a plant than the Chinese; seldom reaching 30 feet. Another interesting difference is that the Chinaman twines clockwise and the Jap counter-clockwise.

W. venusta about matches *floribunda* for vigour and bears white flowers in bunches that are about half the size of those of *sinensis.*

The name "Wisteria" is a slight curiosity. It was named after Professor Caspar Wistar, of Pennsylvania University but in the official registration the *a* became an *e,* so "wisteria" it officially remains.

WOODBINE. See "Honeysuckle".

CHAPTER 8

WALL SHRUBS

Of course, almost any shrub can be planted against a wall or fence, but what we are concerned with in this book are shrubs of two main sorts: those that are generally hardy but particularly suitable for displaying on walls and those that, in most localities, need the warmth and comfort of a wall of some sort.

The latter category, which includes many shrubs we ardently desire, heavily outnumber the former, alas, and we shall find all too many that have to be confined to those Gulf Stream counties of which we have already heard a good deal and which, as before, we shall label with the symbol §. Plenty are borderline cases and more still will succumb in a frost pocket in even the more pampered counties. And I would remind the reader that hardiness, meaning here frost-hardiness, is a relative quality and a plant that may die in one spot may live in another a few miles, or even a few yards away.

Wind, water and shade also come into the reckoning. Strong winds, especially salty winds, may severely strain a plant's resistance; lack of summer rain and atmospheric moisture may cast it into the depths of depression; some light, dappled shade overhead will take a little of the sting out of the sharp stabs of frost. We should remember also those few Chilean splendours, discussed in pages 7–8, that expect both warmth and shade and thus may be difficult to place – the berberidopsis, the desfontainea, the crinodendron and others.

Besides those that I have included in this chapter, there are quantities of other tender shrubs that can be grown only in the warm, moist coastal gardens (or in greenhouses), but a limit must be set to one's pages, so I confine myself to what seem to be the most desirable and the least exacting. Whenever there is a doubt about frost hardiness, take the precaution of covering the plant's crown and roots with a thick quilt of leaves or bracken held in place by a cage of wire netting, and envelop the upper structure in thick sacking. In more extreme cases the whole thing may be wrapped up in straw, but this sometimes introduces complications.

Gardeners with a little experience, a good eye and a gleam of imagination may by the use of wall shrubs achieve the happiest unions between house and garden. In many an old cottage one has seen how the skilled gardener of other days, with a sureness of touch that few but he possessed, has planted yew or box on either side of his front door, forming buttresses which perfectly suit the architecture and add solidity and even a touch of mystery to the humble entrance. Very often he has grown these shrubs right over the door, to form a deep, cavernous porch.

We could with great advantage imitate this excellent example in many of our new and immature houses, especially those raw and depressing structures that we have come to associate with the idea of "council houses". To form these buttresses and porches, as well as socles or plinths beneath windows, we could today very well use the pyracantha and the ceanothus in place of the slower growing yew and box.

In cities and in industrial towns it is usually safest, unless one is prepared to give the evergreens frequent hosings, to use deciduous shrubs. There are plenty of them, including the bone-hardy flowering quince and the forsythia, the nearly hardy abutilons and a great many that are of Gulf Stream disposition. In this chapter we shall also meet the jasmine and that engaging flopper, the solanum.

Several of the plants in this chapter will need a certain amount of tailoring to fit them to the wall. In particular, the pyracantha, the flowering quince and the ceanothus, which ought to hug their walls closely, may be trained in a manner similar to the espalier apple, though not necessarily with the same rigidity of rule. Various other designs of the fruit fancier may also be copied – single, double and quadruple cordons, gridirons and so on. There are few quicker ways of covering an expanse of wall with decorative evergreen than planting a row of cordon pyracanthas, 15 inches or so apart, as seen at Exbury.

Abelia

The abelias are a charming, graceful family whose slender, arching stems are clothed with small, glossy leaves and generously strung with small, pretty bells in pink or white. They are mostly deciduous and only half-hardy, though the best known one, which is the evergreen *A. grandiflora*, seems to be hardy enough in the open in all but the coldest regions. In accord with her usual habit of vexing or challenging us, nature tries to keep the more charming ones out of our reach, but we can often defeat her with a nice warm wall.

For this use the following are the most desirable species:

A. floribunda §. The most beautiful of all and the least hardy, needing wall protection almost anywhere. Slender, pendulous trumpets of warm rose-red, nearly 2 inches long, dangle in thick clusters on its lax stems among small, lustrous leaves in June and July. In the west of Scotland and in Cornwall it may grow 15 feet high and behave as an evergreen, but in the south of England, in the London area and in the home counties it is unlikely to reach half that height and may lose some or all of its leaves.

A. schumannii, a favourite of mine, is not nearly so difficult to please and will probably reward the gardener anywhere if given a warm wall or fence, while in the southern and western counties it will grow well in the open. It is flowered with pretty, small bells of soft rose-pink, which ornament the elegant stems throughout the whole summer and well into the autumn. It is deciduous and on a wall will reach to about 6 feet.

A. grandiflora, the most widely grown and an extremely fine shrub, with very small pallid pink bells among small, glittering evergreen leaves, needs wall protection only in the coldest counties.

All these abelias seem to be quite content with a good, loamy soil. The only pruning needed is to remove old branches at full length from time to time.

Abeliophyllum

A charming little deciduous shrub, but a slow mover. Imagine a forsythia wreathed in blush-pink florets, waning almost to white, enlivened by the bright little golden eye of its stamens, and almond scented to boot, and you have *A. distichum* (the only species). The plant is quite hardy, but the buds make bold to challenge the frosts of February and in some seasons pay the penalty; so protection from the north and east by a wall, fence, or hedge is a wise precaution. The shrub has a twiggy habit and is not often seen more than four feet high but it may go to six. The flowers come mostly on last year's shoots, which should accordingly be pruned back rather more than half-way immediately after flowering. Any reasonable soil will do, but not a red brick background.

Abutilon

The abutilons that we know are slender, graceful shrubs, or sometimes small trees, with vine-like foliage and with flowers that often resemble those of the mallow or hollyhock. None is fully hardy in the open except in the favoured counties, but there are a few that will handsomely decorate a south wall in most parts of the country.

A. vitifolium is the best known and the hardiest, equipped to grow as an open-ground shrub in the west and parts of the south and well qualified as a wall shrub in others. It is a beautiful plant, wind-resistant, growing maybe to twelve feet or so in normal conditions, with grey-green leaves shaped very like those of a vine (as its name suggests) and decorated abundantly with mallow-like flowers of soft lilac in June and July. There is an equally beautiful white form and a particularly charming new variety named 'Veronica Tennant', with petals faintly flushed a tender, mallow-pink which emphasize the orange anthers and the little purple style.

When really happy *A. vitifolium* develops a tree-like habit and is spoilt if it has to be cut back or required to stick close to a wall; so it should have plenty of room and be well away from any path. A good shrub for seaside gardens.

A. megapotamicum § is a much more exotic creature that immediately draws all eyes, but, in accordance with nature's usual rules, it is far less hardy. Only in the most cosseted counties will it attempt to grow in the open, but will make a brave show on a warm wall in the temperate ones (as in England south of the Thames) but in others usually has to be nursed in a greenhouse.

It is a slender and graceful shrub, seldom exceeding 4 feet, quite amenable to being tied close back to the wall, with leaves tapering to a long, fine point. From this structure it dangles long, pendulous, showy flowers having very large and bold calyces of bright red, from which protrude the yellow, half-expanded petals of the flower, themselves extruding bold bosses of stamens and purple stigmas.

You may imagine it as a tiny doll in red blouse and yellow petticoat; or it may suggest the "poke-bonnets" of the Regency, as worn by a bold hussy. Like bold hussies, it is also very persistent in its display, flowering at unexpected times, and its best floral efforts seem to be encouraged by a poor, stony soil. There is a variety with mottled foliage that I do not care for.

Ashfold Red is a fine, showy variety with quite large flowers of dusky red, which are rather bells than "poke-bonnets", and with fine-pointed leaves. Rather lax of habit, it is best tied back loosely to the wall or fence to make a good display.

Golden Fleece is much the same and just as good as 'Ashfold Red' but with clear lemon-yellow flowers and larger leaves.

A. milleri brings us back to the poke-bonnet, with apricot petals protruding from prominent, light brown calyces.

Berberidopsis §

One of the most beautiful of all wall shrubs is *B. corallina*, sometimes called the "coral plant". Wherever it can be grown well its superlative display enriches the scene with pendulous clusters of twenty or more raspberry-sized flowers of a rich, deep-red – "coral-red" it was said, but more nearly blood-red or crimson, richer than rubies. These jewels the plant begins to expose in July and it keeps its exhibition open all the rest of the summer and into September.

The berberidopsis is a slender, scrambling, half-hardy shrub clothed in darkly evergreen leaves with spiny points resembling those of the berberis and so accounting for its name. It needs a square yard or more of acid soil when it is planted but, after it is established, has no objection to pushing its roots out into a limy one. What it seems to prefer is one which is rather light and rather sandy in texture.

It enjoys a damp atmosphere and so can be grown in the sun in such climates as Cornwall, south Devon, north Wales and western Scotland, but elsewhere must have some shade to prevent excessive transpiration. Thus in mild climates it may be grown on a northerly wall, but in cooler ones a south wall shaded by adjacent trees seems better and in these shadowy places the colour gains in splendour. A west wall is a good compromise.

In nature the berberidopsis is a lax scrambler over other shrubs (a purpose for which it can be equally well used in the mild climates here), so that, when grown on a wall, the shoots must be tied up to a wire grid or to nails until it is full-grown, after which it can be left to grow at will.

Calceolaria §

Calceolarias are familiar to all gardeners for their inflated, pouchy petals of those sorts grown for summer bedding or for the greenhouse. Less familiar is the gay and very long-flowering shrub, *C. integrifolia*, which flourishes in the open ground in the west and in the sunniest parts of the south, but which, in climates such as that of London, needs a warm wall plus winter protection. It well repays this small attention wherever it has a chance, for it is so lively a plant and so generous, blooming from midsummer right through till the end of September. Some sacking or a thick quilt of leaves, caged in by wire netting, usually suffices. Moreover, it is suitable to the smallest wall or fence, taking up little more than 4 feet.

This calceolaria is an evergreen, with rough, sage-like leaves and very large trusses crowded with many small yellow flowers, which have the typical calceolaria form of a pouchy lower petal and a small, snub-nosed upper one.

CAPE FIGWORT. See *Phygelius capensis*.

Camellia

If they were a little cheaper and a little quicker off the mark, camellias would, I am sure, be among our most popular shrubs, abounding in the gardens of cottage and castle alike. Given a lime-free soil, plenty of moisture and a little shade, they are so easy to grow.

The hardiest breeds are the innumerable varieties of *C. japonica* and the small group of the new and sun-hardy hybrid *C. williamsii* – all creations of the most appealing beauty.

There is no need at all to give these wall protection, except perhaps in the bitterest corners of the country, and they positively dislike a south wall, for they like things cool, moist and shady. These hardy sorts are accordingly outside our brief.

Other species of camellia are certainly less hardy and need frost protection away from the west and south. These include the many varieties of the magnificent *C. reticulata*, with its large, net-veined leaves, the beautiful pink *saluenensis*, and the sweet-scented, winter-flowering, delicately tinted *sasanqua* (which will succeed in full sun).

These and other species are quite happy in the open in the more favoured districts, but elsewhere must have some protection. They make extremely handsome adornment for a wall, even when out of flower, for their form and foliage put most other plants metaphorically into the shade; they are certainly more handsome out of flower than many rhododendrons.

Away from the western and southern coasts the best walls are usually those that face west or north-west, where they will get some warmth and not too much sun. In the warm counties they are highly successful on north walls.

Apart from an acid soil and shade for the sun-tender species, the prime need of the camellia is water, especially during the summer, when next year's buds are forming, and during the spring, when the big fat buds are ready to open. These buds often fall in the most distressing manner, the causes of which are attributable to one or other of the following factors:

waterlogging of the roots;
any sudden climatic change, such as:
heavy rain following a drought,
a sudden frost after a mild spell,
in easterly exposures a sudden thaw.

We can provide against the first two causes at least by ensuring good drainage and by seeing that there is no period of drought.

Of the many ***reticulata*** varieties, one has only to pick one's preferences for colour or form, but most people would have no hesitation about going straight for 'Captain Rawes', long-known as 'Semiplena', which bursts out into superlative, semi-double flowers of a rich rose-red, often nearly 6 inches wide. On very small plants these huge blossoms may look a little odd, but time soon puts things into proper proportions.

C. saluenensis is, of course, a true species, but there are various colour forms.

C. sasanqua and its varieties have never been very high in the popularity polls, for they flower well in only the most genial localities.

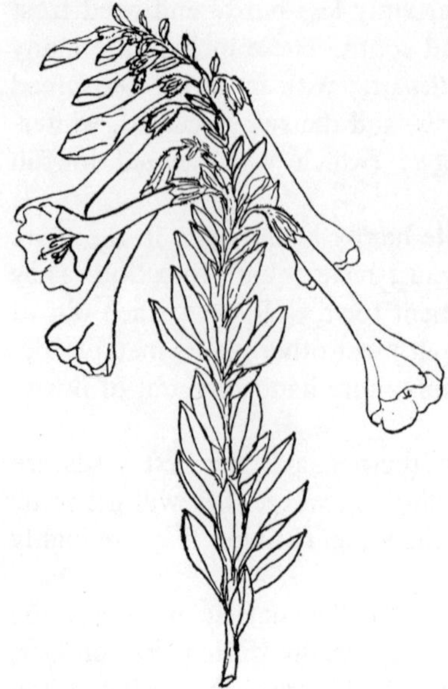

FIG. 19. *Cantua buxifolia*

Cantua §

Even Bean from his Olympian height apostrophizes *C. buxifolia* (or *dependens*) as a "gorgeous shrub". It is one which in April and May bursts out from coiled, bright red buds into pendulous clusters of trumpets, 3 inches long, in a brilliant colour arrangement of many shades of red, but with deep rose predominating, and yellow within the throat.

Only rarely in this country, however, is it truly "gorgeous". Even in the Gulf Stream counties it must have a hot wall. It seldom flowers freely and its proper place is in a cool greenhouse, where it becomes much more obliging and will make a highly decorative display if its shoots are trained up towards the roof.

Carpenteria

Carpenteria californica is a neat and decorative evergreen shrub bearing, in June and July, immaculate white flowers in the style of single roses. It used to be considered tender, but the record freeze-up of 1963 showed it to be hardy in many parts of the country. In the cooler counties, however, a wall is no doubt advisable. My own

FIG. 20. *Carpenteria californica.*

plants, 4 foot high after five years, have never yet flowered, so have nearly all been fired, but it is one of the most beautiful of shrubs in other people's gardens.

Cape Figwort

(*Phygelius capensis*)

This is an architecturally decorative plant, in which the flower stalks are curved and the tubular flowers themselves, like elegant little hunting-horns, are slightly curved also, but in the opposite direction. They dangle in tiers on the spire-like stems in early autumn.

The cape figwort, although a South African, is nearly hardy in this country, but outside the favoured climes must be grown against

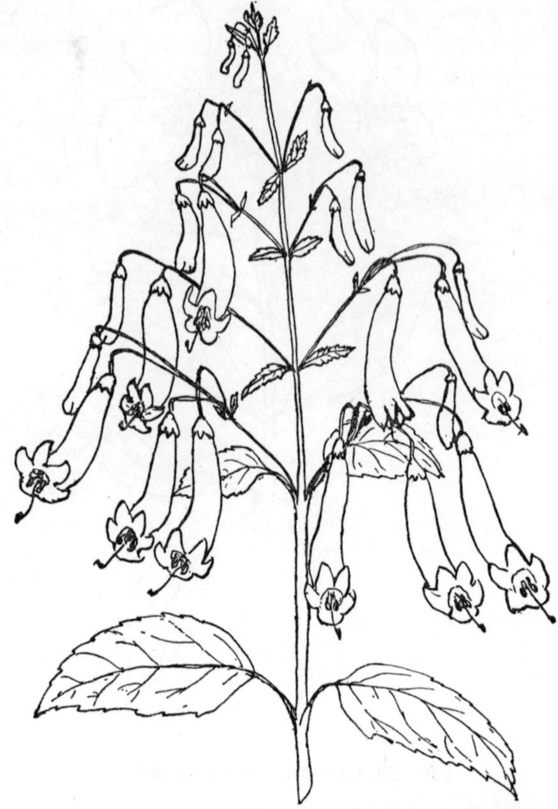

Fig. 21. The Cape figwort, *Phygelia capensis.*

a wall, where it is reported to be capable of reaching 20 feet, though 6 or 7 feet is more usual. It is a semi-herbaceous plant, so that if the top growth is killed by frost, new growths shoot from the ground, provided that the crown of the plant and the root area have been protected by a thick blanket of caged-in leaves. It is content with a rather poor, stony soil. The best variety is 'Coccinea', in which the flowers are a bright scarlet.

Ceanothus

The ceanothus is one of our most valued garden shrubs. Its foliage alone, usually small and very dense, is handsome and when it becomes animated with a haze of little fluffy blue tuffets it provides an element that is particularly well suited to the British scene, yet one which no other shrub adequately presents. The colours range from lively, bright blues, through rich dark ones, pallid wood-smoke ones, lavender and even one or two pinks and whites.

All of the ceanothuses grown in Britain are on the borderline of hardiness – some just on the safe side, others a little on the wrong one. There is a fairly clear divide and the touchstone is provided, in general terms, by the season of flowering. There are two main groupings. The first comprises early-flowering evergreens and the second late-flowering deciduous ones.

The deciduous sorts are sufficiently hardy to be grown in the open in most parts of the country and will call for a protective hedge, wall or fence only where the frost is the sharpest and the atmosphere the driest. Therefore we shall not be concerned with them in this book, except to make passing mention of such leading varieties as the celebrated 'Gloire de Versailles', 'Topaz' and the pink 'Marie Simon' and 'Perle Rose'. They flower in late summer and autumn.

The evergreens, however, are all somewhat on the tender side, will grow in the open only in the more temperate climates and in other parts of the country call for a wall or fence, for which they provide one of our handsomest adornments. They flower in spring, mostly in May, and they make particularly good seaside plants.

This division is a generalization to which there are the usual exceptions, such as the late-flowering evergreens 'Autumnal Blue' and *burkwoodii*, and any classification is confounded when we meet 'A. T. Johnson', which flowers both early and late.

Except for the slight pruning problem when grown on a wall, the ceanothus is a pretty easy plant when once established, after which it grows away very fast. There are, however, a few special likes and dislikes to be emphasized. Its fleshy and brittle roots dislike movement, so it must be bought in a pot. Planting must always be done in spring, for even the hardiest, such as *C. thyrsiflorus*, are frost-tender when very young and, if planted in autumn, will succumb in the first winter unless it is a mild one. All seem to be largely indifferent to their soil but probably flower best on poor, stony ones or sandy, seaside ones, rather than fat loams (though mine have always done well in rich soils). Good drainage is mightily important.

Unhappily, ceanothus are often short-lived. After about nine years, sometimes less, they seem to funk the frost and may give up the ghost in a hardish winter. However, they grow so very fast that a new plant will quickly make good the casualty.

When it is grown on a wall, the ceanothus needs a little training and pruning. Build up a basic framework, fanning the strongest branches well out and tying them fairly close to the wall. During this process and subsequently, pruning is governed by the fact that the evergreens (with such exceptions as we shall note) bring forth their flowers on the "old wood" grown the previous summer. This means in theory shearing hard back the shoots that have flowered to a couple of buds from the main branches and this is done immediately flowering is finished.

I don't myself like defoliating a shrub to this extent all at one go, and accordingly I prefer to cut back half-way at first and to complete the business a week or so later. The few evergreens that break the rules and flower in late summer or autumn are better pruned back in April (like the deciduous ones).

Most ceanothus species come from the United States, particularly from California, but, in addition to these species, there are now some fine hybrids at our disposal. Indeed, "hybrid vigour" has resulted in some of the true species being surpassed for garden value. Thus, while *C. cyaneus* is perhaps the most beautiful of all, it is also the most difficult and, for the practical gardener, perhaps the best "all-rounders" are such hybrids as 'Delight' and 'Autumnal Blue'. For sheer hardiness, however, there is still probably none to beat the old species *thyrsiflorus*.

Here, then, is a fairly long list of the evergreen hybrids to choose from.

A. T. Johnson. A flowerful hybrid with tufts of Wedgwood blue in spring and again in autumn. Fairly hardy and good against a west or south wall.

Autumnal Blue. A pretty hardy *thyrsiflorus* hybrid that can be grown in the open in most districts but stands a better chance in the colder ones if protected. It is clothed with large, glossy, oval leaves and persistently pushes out quantities of large trusses of light blue from the middle of July till the end of September. Discourage any inclination to spring flowering by pruning hard back in April.

C. burkwoodii Offspring of a union between a spring evergreen species and an autumn deciduous variety, this ceanothus tries to imitate both parents. This results in its blooming over the same period as 'Autumnal Blue', but in being not quite evergreen in all climates. Its bold panicles of flowers are of a rich, deep blue. It is only tolerably hardy and is best on a sunny wall, where it will reach to fifteen feet. Prune in April.

Cascade. This is a variety or hybrid of *thrysiflorus* and so nearly hardy. It has an easy, arching habit and when grown in the open is a magnificent fountain of soft blue, the flowers being borne abundantly in fluffy clusters. On a wall it will shoot up to 20 feet and makes a bushy plant, growing outwards. Very effective if given ample room.

Delight. A splendid hybrid and one of the hardiest, needing wall protection only in the coldest places. Viewed from a little distance, the whole shrub is a haze of blue, soft yet brilliant. The dense foliage is made up of small, dark, glistening leaves. It grows very fast on a wall and will soon reach 20 feet.

C. dentatus. One of the best known species of ceanothus, being composed of small, densely crowded, bright green leaves with rolled margins and set about with innumerable little powder puffs of light blue in May. It is a good plant for the seaboard, but is hardy in the milder districts only unless given wall protection. The species itself is equalled or surpassed by some of its varieties and hybrids, which include:

> 'Floribundus', long familiar in Britain as a wall shrub and larger and showier in all its parts than the species, being splendidly arrayed with dense clusters of pure powder blue.
>
> 'Russellianus', a very decorative hybrid of slightly looser habit with bright blue tufts. It will reach 15 feet and is of bushy habit, growing away from the wall after a year or two and needing plenty of room.

C. impressus is a species that has deeply impressed leaves on arching stems, with pink buds that open bright blue. Particularly good for a small wall area, which should be a sunny one.

Dignity is another of the few autumn-flowering evergreen varieties, and a very good one, too, with delightful florets of a clear blue on large spikes. It is hardy enough in the open in most areas. On a wall, prune in April.

C. papillosus definitely needs a wall in most places. It is a handsome shrub with long, arching, branches, long narrow leaves and small tufts of blue-mauve. It grows to 15 feet or more on a wall. Its variety *roweanus* is beautiful and distinctive, with deep blue flowers, and deeply channelled leaves.

C. rigidus. Another of the leading species and in most areas quite safe on a wall, for which purpose it is widely used, being easy to train. A good seaboard plant for sandy soils in the warmer counties. It flowers in early spring. The very small and attractive leaves are densely crowded on stiff branches and the plant is sheeted in small trusses of bright indigo tinted with mauve. The variety *pallens* is a paler colour, preferred by some people.

C. thyrsiflorus. Probably the hardiest of all, this old species needs a wall in none but the chilliest areas, where it is most impressive. It is, however, not much use on a small house or other wall, for it has tree-like proportions and will grow to 30 feet. Its glossy leaves are accompanied by compound flower clusters up to 3 inches long in lovely shades of blue, according to strain.

C. veitchianus. A natural hybrid that is fairly hardy only in the west, south and home counties (except in frost pockets), but elsewhere makes a fine wall plant, being amenable to training and hard pruning. It flowers with great freedom in clusters of bright blue and is in general pretty reliable, attaining some 10 feet.

CHAENOMELES. See Flowering Quince.

Clianthus §

The "parrot's bill" or "lobster claw", which is *Clianthus puniceus*, is a gorgeous plant for the favoured few or for the adventurous. The "favoured few" here means, as so often, those who live in the Gulf Stream regions. The "adventurous" means those living a little inland in the south and west with warm, south-facing walls or south-west inglenooks, but they must cover the plant with a thick mat if hard frost threatens.

Normally a floppy shrub in its native New Zealand, this clianthus, where its wants are satisfied, may grow 15 feet high on a wall, luxuriantly clad in small ferny foliage and showered with pendulous, opulent clusters of the most vivid red imaginable. The bizarre flowers of the clusters have a vague resemblance to either a parrot's bill or a lobster's claw, according to which way you look at them and how exquisite is your imagination. In fact they are exaggerated pea-flowers, but a great deal larger, having a "standard" nearly 2 inches high and an even longer "keel", which is curved and sharply pointed.

Nothing in the flower world is more dazzling and it may be seen decorating many houses in Cornwall.

The plant is evergreen and the graceful, frond-like foliage is elegant at all seasons. Flowering begins in June and goes on for a long time. The most suitable soil is an open, sandy loam. Where the clianthus cannot be grown outdoors, it is an easy plant for any greenhouse, even one with no heat.

There is a white variety, *albus*, obviously less showy.

Clianthus formosus (or *dampieri*), the so-called "glory pea", is a warm greenhouse plant and not an easy one at that.

Corokia

These very distinctive New Zealanders, so useful to the flower arranger, are fully hardy in the Gulf Stream areas and almost anywhere in the south, but not quite so in the rest of the country. They make "intriguing" shrubs for a south wall or fence and are excellent hosts for climbers of moderate growth, such as the passion flower and the clematis 'Hagley Hybrid'. They are small-leaved evergreens and are notably wind-hardy. Any good soil suits them. The usual species are:

C. cotoneaster, sometimes called the "wire netting bush", because of its wiry, interlacing zigzag branches and twigs – like a large, openwork bird's nest, you might say, if there were such a thing. It is clothed with small, spoon-shaped leaves, seldom grows more than 7 feet high and is smothered in myriads of tiny golden stars in May, followed by little, orange fruits.

C. virgata has much the same sort of flowers and fruits, but not the bird's-nest habit; it grows rather taller and more loosely, with leaves that are white underneath.

Coronilla

Beautiful evergreen shrubs of modest stature, bearing yellow pea-flowers over an exceptionally long span of the year, but needing warmth and shelter in most areas. The best of them is:

C. glauca. A choice shrub, with beautiful, small, pinnate, sea-green leaves and sweetly scented pea-flowers of rich yellow in clusters of six to ten. As charming on a cottage wall as on that of a mansion, providing it has sun. The main flush of its flowers comes in April to May, but in most places it will bloom intermittently all the year and in Cornwall blooms well all the winter. It will reach to 8 feet but can be pruned back if space is limited.

C. valentina is a smaller edition of *glauca,* producing a mass of scented flowers throughout the summer, but perhaps a trifle more tender.

C. emerus, the "scorpion senna", is deciduous and has a ruddy streak in the yellow of the blossom, but is not a patch on the others, though usually hardier.

Cotoneaster

The shrubs and small trees so familiar in our gardens and in the roadside planting of the new "dual carriageways" have some brethren that in nature are of lowly habit but are adept at climbing a wall entirely without support. They are first-rate for small walls and fences, are bone-hardy, not fastidious about the soil and will do well in any aspect.

The most popular is ***C. horizontalis,*** the "herring-bone" cotoneaster. In nature this useful plant fans itself out in a more or less horizontal plane. Planted against a wall, however, it will fan out gracefully in a vertical one, leaning flat against the wall. It will grow, rather slowly, to about 8 feet, or occasionally more, clothed in very small leaves which hang on till about Christmas and massed in autumn with bright red berries after its tiny May flowers. Bees love it. After leaf-fall, or even before, its branch structure shows very clearly its resemblance to the skeleton of a fish.

There is a variety with tiny parti-coloured leaves, very attractive but very slow.

Popular though *horizontalis* is, I prefer the evergreen *microphyllus.* This in nature grows into a shrub about 2 feet high and then sprawls outwards. Against a wall it will behave in much the same way as *horizontalis,* though not in the same fan-like style and with no resemblance to fish bones. It is densely covered with tiny leaves, bursts out into a fuzz of minute flowers in May and June and bears red berries in the autumn. Its leading shoots may need a little initial guidance on to the wall. In the open garden it is a splendid shrub for trailing down over the edge of a terrace or a bank.

Very different from these smaller cotoneasters are those larger species which are usually grown as open-ground shrubs. Some of them, particularly, *C. wardii*, can, with a little skill and care, be built up in about four years to very fine fan-trained wall shrubs, either formal or informal. One very formal method is as follows.

After the young plant has had a full season to get itself established, lead out the strongest branches fan-wise and tie them to long canes radiating in the desired directions and fastened to the grid or trellis on the wall. Cut out all outward-growing breastwood and all shoots growing inwards to the wall.

Next winter prune back all the branches by not less than one-third, cutting just above a good bud. The result in the following summer will be the production of several new shoots from each branch. Lead out the shoot resulting from the top bud in continuation of the line of the branch. Also select three other well-placed buds on each branch to grow on – two on the upper side of each branch and one on the lower. Rub out all other buds. Lead the selected new shoots out symmetrically as further ribs of the fan, tying them to radiating canes as before.

In the following winter cut back all the branches by not less than a third, as before, and in the succeeding summer again select four buds to grow on from each branch. Continue this process until the available space is filled. And see Fig. 27.

Each April prune back the laterals that have fruited to three leaves of their parent branches. The result should be closely knit displays of berries on short spurs, which, of course, the birds will steal from you unless you frustrate them with nets.

Crinodendron §

I wish someone would devise an acceptable vernacular name for this delightful and very ornamental genus, which, having had its name changed from *Tricuspidaria*, has merely been thrown out of the frying-pan into the fire. *Crinodendron*, or "lily tree", is a stupid and inappropriate name. The awful contortions of the names of their species makes things worse for the simple gardener. No wonder that they are not grown as much as they should be.

The crinodendrons are darkly evergreen shrubs which hang their branches with little lanterns or bells in the balmy airs of the west and south and occasionally in sheltered nooks and corners farther inland. It flourishes in Mr R. B. Cooke's garden in Northumberland. A good thick hedge is often sufficient shelter, but they are another of those awkward creatures mentioned in page 7 that expect not only warmth, but also shade, plentiful moisture and a fibrous and acid soil, being immigrants from the forests of Chile. Thus a south wall is not the right thing unless in the shade of other trees. In warm places, north or east walls are the order.

The species usually most favoured is ***C. hookerianum***, a peach of a shrub profusely strung with delightful little crimson Chinese lanterns, which gleam with festival gaiety in May and June in the shade that this species particularly enjoys. In mild areas it should be one of the first choices and in the most fortunate situations, as in Cornwall and the west of Scotland, it will grow up to 20 feet. Cut it back after flowering and you will increase its density. In some reference books this species is said to enjoy the vernacular name of "lantern tree" which would be appropriate enough, but it has no general currency. Its former official name, still used in some catalogues, was *Tricuspidaria lanceolata*, besides others that we had best forget. Poor creature.

The other species grown is ***C. patagua***, which is hung with pretty white bells. It seems to be hardier than *hookerianum*, but shy in displaying its favours. Of its several aliases, the one most commonly used is *Tricuspidaria dependens*.

Daphne

The daphnes are among our most beautiful, most fragrant, but most capricious small shrubs and all are pretty hardy, except the marvellously scented *D. odora*. Planted on a south wall beneath a sitting-room window, it will embalm the air with the sweetest of breaths on the chilliest days in February and March from the clusters of tiny rose-purple florets borne at the ends of its branches. It is handsomely evergreen, grows to about 3 feet only and for effective display is usually tied up to the wall. Very successful in lime soils.

Its variety with yellow-margined leaves, 'Aureo-marginata', is usually considered to be a trifle hardier and is the one usually grown.

Fig. 22. *Desfontainea spinosa.*

Desfontainea §

D. spinosa is a magnificent shrub with holly-like foliage, sprinkled all over with scarlet, or scarlet and gold, trumpets an inch and a half long from July onwards, followed by cherry-like fruits. It grows superbly out in the open in the west of Scotland and in Northern Ireland and very well in parts of Cornwall. Furthermore, it grows splendidly in the Royal Botanic Garden, Edinburgh, and in Mr. R. B. Cooke's Northumberland garden.

There is therefore little support for its reputation for tenderness. The truth, no doubt, is that the desfontainea, coming from the rain forests of Chile, is another of that group of plants discussed on page 7 that require special conditions of soil, situation and climate, given which it will delight the heart. If the climatic conditions are right, it is worth going to a lot of trouble to get the soil right, too.

A lime-free soil is to be preferred but is not essential. See that it has plenty of water and an annual mulch of leaves.

D. hookeri has smaller, darker leaves and a dense growth but seldom seems to flower well.

DRIMYS WINTERI, See Winter's Bark.

Fabiana

The fabianas are evergreen, heather-like shrubs, pretty hardy, growing to perhaps 6 feet (more in Cornwall) and spreading widely. There used to be a fine specimen on the west wall of the Cambridge Botanic Garden, a fact that gives a fair idea of its degree of hardiness; some wall protection would certainly be wise in the colder counties. They are valuable shrubs for chalky soils, but do equally well in acid ones.

Their floral habit is to produce single, small, tubular flowers at the tips of short twigs, but these twigs are so numerous that the bushes become smothered. The leaves are tiny and numerous, obscuring the twigs in the manner of the heathers. They must be cut hard back after flowering (which is in June), otherwise they get fearfully shabby.

The species usually grown are *F. imbricata*, which bears white flowers, and *F. violacea*, which is hardier, stronger growing and bears flowers which may be anything from a washy milk-blue to a good, clear mauve. A good colour strain should be sought, such as that of the Slieve Donard nursery.

Feijoa

Suitable only for large walls, *Feijoa sellowiana* is a big, handsome evergreen shrub which is hardy enough to be grown in Suffolk and at Kew, where there is a fine specimen, but in general it seems to flower best in the Gulf Stream regions. It has decorative grey-green foliage and an ivory felt on the young shoots. The flowers, borne in July, are red and are remarkable for the large brush of crimson stamens that sprout from them, making a brave display. An easy plant to grow in any reasonable soil, with or without lime, if the climate is right.

Flowering Quince

(*Chaenomeles*)

"Flowering quince" and "Japanese quince" (some are Chinese) are much more valid vernacular names for those splendid shrubs that some people still pointlessly call "japonicas". Unfortunately the flowering quince has been the prey of sharp-eyed botanists, who within my lifetime have changed it from *Pyrus* to *Cydonia* and then to *Chaenomeles*. To make things more difficult still for gardeners, they have switched the old epithet *japonica* from one species to another one.

However, the flowering quince itself remains faithful to its sterling character and will never let anyone down. It is among the most beautiful of all shrubs, albeit one of the commonest, and is one of the chief glories of the early spring and even of winter. It is perfectly hardy anywhere, but comes within the scope of this book because one of its species makes a particular fine wall shrub, suitable for gardens of all sorts and sizes and in any part of the country.

This is the species now legally known (its fourth change of name) as *C. speciosa*. It has several very good colour forms and a few others suitable for walls have come to us from its hybrid offspring *superba*. Among them[1] are:

- 'Rosea Plena', rose, double.
- 'Falconnet Charlet', salmon, double.
- 'Moerloosei', pale pink and white.
- 'Nivalis', white.
- 'Boule de Feu', vermilion.

These varieties will, in time, average about 8 or 9 feet in height and rather more in width, but they are easily restrained if necessary. They will succeed in any aspect, being one of the most favoured plants for a north wall, but do best on a south or south-west one, which will bring out their heart-warming flowers at about Christmas-time and keep them going for three months or more. On other walls the season usually starts late in February. They are slightly thorny.

The craft of growing these quinces in full beauty on walls lies in

[1] I have taken these identities and spellings, which differ from those of other publications, from Mr C. D. Brickell, the RHS botanist.

their training and pruning. They are very close cousins of the apple and anyone who has cultivated cordon or espalier apples will know what to do, for they flower on short spurs on shoots one or more years old.

We do not, however, follow the careful precision of the fruit-grower, but use his methods in an informal manner. There are various ways of doing so. One simple one is to grow them as informal espaliers. First build up a basic framework, by running up a leader and training out lateral branches, the while cutting out all outward-thrusting breastwood and shoots growing into the wall. As soon as sub-laterals form, summer prune them at the fifth leaf and winter prune them hard back to the second bud.

This loose espalier form can be varied as you will, as by bringing up more than one leader; or the plant may be trained in any other shape to which the apple is amenable.

By this means you develop a well-tailored shrub, compact, closely hugging the wall and producing quantities of flowers, which, if the branches are cut just before the buds open, will last in winter for ages.

The fruit that results is bitter but edible, with a flavour similar to that of the cultivated quince. It makes excellent quince jelly and a thick slice from one of these fruits adds piquancy to an apple-pie. If brought into the house the fruits will fill a whole room with their aroma, and, if allowed to dry, make amusing rattles for babies, as the flesh shrivels and leaves the pips within the hardened skin.

While the shrub is young, however, the embryo fruit should be picked off as soon as the blossom falls, so that the shrub will put its energies into growth.

The various aliases which have been acquired by *C. speciosa* and any of which may be found in catalogues or other writings are: *Pyrus japonica, Cydonia japonica* and *Chaenomeles lagenaria.* A pretty record.

When looking at catalogues, don't be confused by *Chaenomeles japonica*, long celebrated as "Maule's quince" but now robbed of its association with Mr Maule. This is a perfectly splendid and dashing shrub, but a dwarf, spreading widely, not a wall shrub. This also has a list of aliases that looks like a burglar's record.

Two very fine hybrids to be found in catalogues also have the spreading habit of Maule's quince and so are seen in full beauty as open ground shrubs rather than as wall models. These are the blood-red 'Rowallane', the peach-pink 'Cameo' and the inaptly named 'Knaphill Scarlet', all deriving from the hybrid *superba.* The same restriction applies to the brilliant crimson dwarf 'Simonii', though you may grow them on low walls if you wish.

Forsythia

No doubt here about hardiness. All the forsythias we grow are as hard as nails and their golden bells are one of the great glories of early spring.

The species that grows on walls, fences or pergolas is *F. suspensa*, not because there is anything the least tender about it, but because, like winter jasmine, it is a lax, floppy creature, of which the leading shoots must be tied up as they grow to make a brave display.

This means a certain amount of labour on the gardener's part for, if neglected as it so often is, the shrub soon becomes a tiresome slattern. Besides tying up the leading shoots, it is also important to prune out the flowered ones as soon as they have lost their beauty, which is about the second week in April, cutting each back to two or three buds from its junction with the main branch. The longer this is delayed the poorer will be next year's show.

Treated faithfully, *F. suspensa* will become a fountain of gold perhaps 15 feet high. It enjoys a good, rich loam and loves the sun, yet will also delight the beholder on a north wall. It makes an excellent host for a late-flowering clematis.

There are several good forms of the species and its variety *fortunei.* The most popular is *sieboldii,* but it is so very droopy that it is much more impressive when cascading down a terrace or bank, or when carefully trained out along a pergola. 'Decipiens' is of similar habit. I prefer the form called 'Atrocaulis', whose nearly black stems admirably set off the lemon bells, though maybe they are not quite so generously borne.

Fremontia §

F. californica is a beautiful, evergreen, tender shrub, with shapely foliage and embellished with large, golden saucers of waxen texture all through the summer, looking rather like a sublimated St John's

Wort. It is seldom long-lived and, away from the favoured west, needs a warm, sunny nook, where, barring a very severe winter, it may with luck grow to 10 feet. It flowers best in poor, sandy soil and resents root disturbance, so must be obtained in a pot.

F. mexicana is even less hardy.

Garrya

Garrya elliptica is a quick-growing evergreen shrub that is hardy enough for a warm wall almost anywhere. It is grown especially for its fascinating clusters of long, dangling, grey-green, silky catkins, which are borne in the winter and sway about prettily in the cold wind, until the distaff side feloniously gathers them for a flower arrangement. Garryas are unisexual, however, and you must be sure of getting a male plant, for the catkins of the female are not impressive.

Growing some 10 feet high, the shrub is of graceful habit, though a bit sombre in summer and decidedly tatty in a hard winter. It will do well in any aspect but in northern counties a south wall is safest. A good plant for larger places, but for smaller ones there are better things.

G. thuretii is a very fast-growing evergreen of no floral value.

Grevillea §

These Australasians cannot be expected to be tough enough for our country generally, but there are a few that reward the gardener in favoured spots in Sussex and all counties west. They are characterized by very small leaves, sometimes needle-like, and small tubular flowers, superficially like those of the honeysuckle, with a very prominent style ingeniously protruding from a lateral opening in the tube. They are plants for full sun and an acid or neutral soil. Many are capricious. The following are perhaps the most reliable.

G. rosmarinifolia. A 6-foot shrub with foliage like that of rosemary and with small, rose-red flowers carried in densely crowded clusters over a long period.

G. sulphurea is of about the same size, but has pale gold flowers among densely set, needle-like (and needle-sharp) foliage.

G. thyrsoides is very like *rosmarinifolia*, with rose-pink flowers, but has longer leaves and a more upright habit.

Hebe

Hebes were formerly included in the great *Veronica* family, but were recently expelled by the botanists and required to set up house on their own. In this instance the separation was a good idea, for, whereas what now remain as veronicas are herbaceous or rock plants, the hebes are shrubs. Some of them are well enough known, but most are on the questionable side of hardiness and the most beautiful of all is the tenderest, though far hardier than its reputation..

This is *H. hulkeana*, a choice and superlative plant which has a good chance of succeeding against a warm wall in all but the colder

FIG. 23. *Hebe hulkeana.*

regions. In such a situation it will grow to about 3 feet, bearing lustrous green leaves and flourishing long, pyramidal trophies, sometimes more than a foot long, composed of innumerable, tiny florets of an enchanting tincture somewhere between lilac and lavender. It flowers throughout May and June and, when happy, throws out its sumptuous panicles in profusion. These should be beheaded after flowering.

The shrub has a floppy habit, so should be tied back to the wall, but not too rigidly. It seems to dislike proximity to the sea, unlike other hebes.

Other and easier hebes can, if desired, be grown on or near a wall, such as 'Great Orme' (a fine fellow), 'Simon Deleaux', 'La Séduisante' and 'Midsummer Beauty', but all except the last will do little more than adorn the footings.

Itea

Itea ilicifolia is an elegant and evergreen shrub with holly-like foliage, festooned with long, pendulous catkin-like streamers of minute, sweetly-scented, green-and-white florets. This display begins in August and goes on for many weeks where the conditions are right; this means a soil that does not dry out and a snug and sunny position in average climates. In the west it may be better still in partial shade.

I. yunnanensis is very similar but has larger leaves and white flowers.

"JAPONICA." See Flowering Quince.

Jasmine

Tender associations surround the jasmine, or jessamine, in song and story, but the poets (who rarely know anything about gardening) never say what species they are apostrophizing, so that one imbibes the idea that all jasmines are rapturously scented, beautiful and easy. This is far from being true, but we shall here confine ourselves to those most to be desired on all counts. Some of them are stem twiners, others just rambling shrubs.

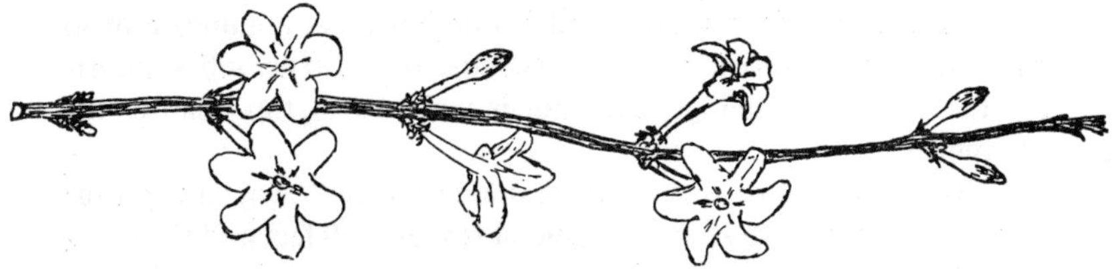

FIG. 24. The winter Jasmine, *Jasminum nudiflorum.*

Easiest of all is the popular, but scentless, winter jasmine, ***Jasminum nudiflorum,*** whose small, naked trumpet-flowers on leafless, green stems sound their cheerful calls in the bleakest months from the walls of many a castle and cottage in the land. It is in no sense whatever a climber, but a wanton flopper and is really at its best when tumbling down a bank or drooping from the edge of a terrace, where it will, moreover, need a minimum of attention by the gardener. When grown in the usual way on a wall it will need quite a lot, if it is not to become the untidy jumble that one so often sees.

Its main shoots should be kept tidily and methodically tied up as they grow to whatever framework has been fixed to the wall and the flowered stems must be pruned back to two or three buds from their junction with the parent stem immediately flowering is over. The new shoots that result from this pruning are the ones that will provide their golden treasury in the next winter and these may well be allowed to flop down in a natural manner. Old and neglected specimens that one may inherit can be cut back as hard as you like, the oldest main stems, if bearing only twiggy little side shoots, being amputated at ground level.

Nicely fanned out, the winter jasmine may cover a space some 10 feet high and more wide. Avoid planting it too close to a path; it is too charming a thing to curse every time you pass, as I have to do. I like best to have it, as I do most winter flowers, where it can be seen from the house and there is no better place for it than around a window.

The winter jasmine is bone-hardy and will succeed in any aspect, including a northerly one, where its brave buds enliven the dark days, but it flowers earlier and better on a south one. Blossom time is largely governed by the weather and in a very cold spell the buds wisely stay closed up. It is a particularly good plant in towns.

J. officinale is the summer jasmine and the jasmine of the *parfumeur*, its glorious scent distilled into bottles at a guinea a drop and a long-loved favourite in our islands. It is a true, self-supporting twiner of scrambling habit, but is included in this chapter for convenience.

Fully hardy in most areas, the summer jasmine is the most vigorous and luxuriant that we know, capable of reaching 30 feet and throwing out shoots that may grow 6 feet in a season. It blooms from midsummer, right through until October, constantly throwing out little clusters of small white trumpets. It is not at its best, in my eyes, on a house wall and is better decorating a pergola or embalming an arbour; or it can be put to scrambling up a tree or over an outhouse. It flowers on the current season's growth and accordingly is pruned in winter and pretty hard if necessary.

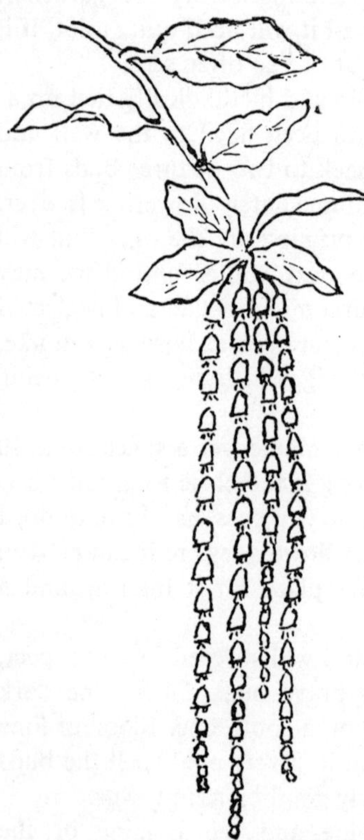

Fig. 25. *Garrya elliptica* (see p. 138).

The form *affine* has larger flowers, tinted pink, and 'Aureo-variegatum' has leaves diversified with cream.

J. primulinum §, the primrose jasmine, is a magnificent but tender evergreen, with flowers of the same fine canary-yellow as the winter jasmine, but much larger and imitating the primrose with widely splayed petals. It blooms in spring, after the winter one has finished, and has no scent. A rambling shrub, it is hardy enough on a warm wall in the south and west, where it attains some 15 feet, but elsewhere will not survive a hard winter. Is now officially *J. mesneyi.*

J. polyanthum §, a twining climber, is more tender still, but survives on warm walls in the west. It is evergreen and very beautiful. The pointed, rose-pink buds open to white, primrose-like flowers, gloriously scented, magnanimously profuse in large, loose panicles. The plant may attain 20 feet.

J. stephanense is a hybrid climber, deciduous, vigorous, fairly hardy and massed with clusters of sweetly scented, small flowers of soft pink, which are followed by glossy, black berries. A pretty jasmine, well suited to pergolas and bowers, but flowering for only two or three weeks from the end of June and never making a really good show. It can be expected to stretch out to a good 15 feet.

Prune all jasmines by cutting back the flowered shoots: the winter and spring species as soon as they have finished flowering, the late ones in February.

See also Chapter 10 for greenhouse jasmines.

KOWHAI. See Sophora, in this chapter.

Lemon-Scented Verbena §

(*Aloysia triphylla* but better known as *Lippia citriodora*)

Of all the plants whose leaves one loves to pluck and crush for their sweet odours as one passes, none is more ambrosial than the lemon verbena. Known previously as *Verbena triphylla*, it subtly combines the aromas of both the verbena and the lemon, breathing, as it might have seemed to Keats, "of the warm south and sunburnt mirth".

Unfortunately for the colder counties, it is the warm south that it prefers, but it will be content enough in average climates if it can bask in sunburnt mirth on a hot wall. We grew it in our wartime garden in the eastern Mendips, where the winters can be infernally cold. One thinks of it as a favourite of old southern cottage gardens, snugly esconced in an outdoor ingle-nook and stroking every passer-by with its slender, scented leaves. It will grow in the open in the very mildest places, where it will develop into a small tree. In doubtful climates it can be grown in a large pot and put into the greenhouse for the winter.

The lemon-scented verbena is deciduous and is not often seen growing more than 10 feet high. It is shrubby, not comfortable or comely if manacled back to the wall. It flowers in August, bearing slender panicles of small, tubular, pale purple florets, which will take no prizes.

Leptospermum §

Evergreen, small-leaved, sparkling with clusters of small, jewel-like flowers, the leptospermums of Australasia are charming shrubs for sheltered places. Dressed in white, pink or red, the little flowers closely hug their stems and individually have the shape, let us say, of minute wild roses. They are seldom more than half an inch wide. The leaves are of about the same size and many of them are dotted with aromatic oil glands, which, it is said, led Captain Cook's sailors to make a brew from them in the manner of tea, so that to this day they are often called "tea trees".

In Britain, those that can be grown outdoors are most likely to be seen in the balmy airs of the Gulf Stream counties, but they also succeed in such latitudes as those of mid-Sussex and Winchester, when given a warm exposure, sheltered by a wall or tall hedge. I associate them most with light, rather sandy soils, though the species most widely grown here (*L. scoparium*) is said to grow naturally in heavy clay in New Zealand. Their roots are hungry and wide-spreading.

Some species are liable to be killed in a hard winter even in our milder counties, but those that seem to offer the best promise are:

L. scoparium. This is the New Zealand "tea tree" of Cook's sailors (though, of course, it has nothing to do with the real tea, which is a camellia species). It may grow to 15 feet where it is happy and there are many beautiful varieties that flower in May and June, but, as it ages, it is apt to become bare and leggy at the base.

FIG. 26. *Leptospermum scoparium.*

The most celebrated is the rosy-carmine 'Nicholsii'; but others just as good are the deep red, double 'Red Damask', the bright rose 'Chapmanii', the pale pink 'Boscawenii', the double white 'Flore Pleno', and the pretty white 'Eximium'.

L. liversidgei is the "lemon-scented tea tree", the minute, crowded leaves having the aroma of lemons when crushed. This is one of the hardiest species, characterized by slender, arching sprays of greenywhite florets. This is a much smaller bush, probably not exceeding 6 feet and not so well adapted, I think, to the confines of a wall.

L. pubescens is another of the hardier species, growing erectly to about 10 feet or so, with downy shoots, silken, silvery leaves and white flowers in June and July. A more ornamental shrub than the former.

LOBSTER CLAW. See *Clianthus puniceus*.

Magnolia

The only magnolia habitually grown against a wall is the splendid *M. grandiflora*. There is little cultural reason for growing it thus, for it is perfectly hardy in most places and makes a magnificent open-ground tree, with its superb, polished, evergreen foliage.

However, it does fit against a wall very snugly, where it has the trick of becoming one with the architecture, and in the colder areas a wall is certainly advisable. On the other hand, it is too often seen on the walls of very small houses, which it will in due time completely swamp. An expansive wall is its demand, with a good 25 feet of headroom and no windows in its 15-foot wide upward path. Though it will grow in any exposure, it produces most flowers on a southerly one.

Of the several varieties of *M. grandiflora*, the finest is 'Goliath', but 'Exmouth' and 'Ferruginea' are very close runners-up. If bought from a nursery of high standing, all will flower when young. When they do appear, the huge, creamy-white goblets, gorgeously scented, are a stunning spectacle and at all times of the year the plant is one of the finest of evergreens.

Another one sometimes grown on a wall is *M. delavayi*. This also is a splendid evergreen species, with very large leaves more than a foot long. Its dull, cream flowers are disappointing and it is grown chiefly for its impressive foliage. It develops into a large, widely spreading plant, which needs a big, blank wall. It is not hardy outside the warm counties, but appears to be a good plant for chalky areas.

All magnolias have sensitive roots, which, after planting, must not be disturbed nor fretted by spade or fork. They must have abundant water, especially in their first season and ought to be thickly mulched with leaves every autumn.

Myrtle

(*Myrtus*)

Beautiful, historic, evergreen shrubs, beloved of the poets. You will remember how Milton came out "to shatter their leaves before the mellowing year". We still today like to shatter them in the hand in order to savour their aroma.

Myrtus communis. the common myrtle, is the one to have for preference, and you may have it in all but the colder counties, if you have a snug south wall. It does well enough in the London area. It may get cut back by frost in a severe winter, but comes on again.

On average, the myrtle grows to about 8 feet (more in warm spots) and is clothed with small leaves of a lustrous dark green, frothing with a profusion of little, sweetly scented, white flowers that have a dense, fluffy brush of stamens protruding from the petals in the manner of the rose of Sharon. The flowers appear in July and August and in a warm summer are followed by handsome little fruits of dusky purple. In a bleak exposure the shrub is apt to look a bit tatty in winter.

The common myrtle has a few very good varieties. Outstanding among them is 'Tarentina' (also known as 'Jenny Reitenbach'), which is a compact little charmer, with a beautiful pattern of small leaves, wind-hardy and a delightful plant beside a door or window on a sunny wall.

There is also a myrtle with variegated foliage and the variety 'Leucocarpa' has white fruits.

There are several other species of myrtle, but all of them are for the cosiest counties only. In Cornwall they seed themselves as readily as the oak and the ash and grow like trees. Thus *M. luma* § is, in fact, the "tree myrtle", a tree of superlative beauty, with a gleaming cinnamon trunk beneath the snow-like canopy of its multitudinous little flowers.

Then there are *M. ugni*, the "Chilean guava", about 5 feet high and having juicy fruits which are edible, *bullata*, with rufous, puckered leaves, not very flowerful, the decidedly tender *lechleriana*, tree-like, with splendid foliage effects in colour, *obcordata*, with minute, reversed-heart shaped leaves, and a few others.

Penstemon §

The penstemons of the herbaceous border and the rock garden are familiar to most gardeners, but the shrubby ones are less well known. One of the best is *P. cordifolius*, a low, lax but pretty shrub to plant beneath a window on a warm wall in a mild district, where it will grow to about 4 feet. It is evergreen and the handsome scarlet flowers are of typical penstemon form – tubular with pouting lips – and are on display from midsummer till autumn. The shoots need tying back to the wall, being rather floppy, and should be cut back moderately hard in April.

PHYGELIUS. See Cape Figwort.

Pyracantha

Here we have the perfect wall-hugging shrub, willing to be exactly tailored to corners and curves and to be led round windows and doors, densely evergreen, smothered with a fuzz of white or cream flowers in June and crowded with red or yellow berries in autumn. With one or two exceptions, the pyracanthas are perfectly hardy and will, as far as I know, flourish anywhere in the country and in any reasonable soil and on any wall, though in the north and east the warmer walls are to be preferred in order to ripen the wood and produce a good crop of berries. They can, of course, perfectly well be grown in their natural form of open-ground shrubs, but with that we are not concerned.

On a wall or fence the pyracantha (or "firethorn" if you like) is best trained as an informal espalier, not in the rigid manner of an apple or pear. Run up a main shoot and allow lateral branches to grow out from it every foot or so, training them horizontally. Tie all in fairly closely and flat to the wall. Rub out all other buds or incipient young shoots, particularly the breastwood shoots and those growing inwards to the wall.

Horizontal shoots growing beneath windows can, if you like, be led upwards on reaching the other side of the window. Indeed, the pyracantha lends itself willingly to almost any pattern. It can be led round porches or grown as tall single cordons between pairs of windows. It can form double or triple cordons or many-pronged toasting forks or very long espaliers against a fence.

In April prune back all the sub-laterals that have finished fruiting to within about 3 inches of their parent branches. The result should be a tightly packed display of fruit on very short spurs. Be prepared for the fact that in autumn the birds may rob you of the berries, especially the red ones, but you can defeat them with a neatly arranged net.

Easily the favourite pyracantha for cloaking a wall is ***P. coccinea* 'Lalandii'**; this has neat leaves and orange berries, which are in their full pride in late September and which will hang on the bush until February if not all gobbled up by the birds. It is very amenable to pruning and can grow to 20 feet and more in time. The species itself, *P. coccinea*, is also good, with smaller, red berries.

P. rogersiana is a plant of rather more refinement and much less vigour, seldom exceeding twelve feet. It is clothed with very small, glossy leaves and brings forth small berries with extravagant profusion in diverse shades of yellow and near red, or of bright yellow in the fine variety 'Flava'. This I find to be the most attractive species. Like other yellow-fruited shrubs, it is usually avoided or left till last by the birds.

P. atalantioides (synonym, *P. gibbsii*) is the most vigorous of all the firethorns and will suit a large wall, where, rather late in autumn, it will erupt into a sheet of red berries. It keeps its fruits longer than other species, supposedly because the birds are not so keen on them.

P. angustifolia is less hardy than any of the others, yet seems to endure the climates of the north and east when on a warm wall. Its handsome leaves are very narrow, with a hint of grey from the downy reverse, and orange fruits which usually succeed in hanging on beyond Christmas.

Pyracanthas are occasionally attacked by the apple scab disease, which is evidenced by small, black, hard, dry patches developing with cracks and distortions of the fruit, a rough and broken surface on the twigs and black spots on the leaves. If it occurs, spray before blossoming with lime-sulphur at the rate of one pint to five gallons of water and at half that strength after flowering.

QUINCE. See Flowering Quince.

Solanum

The climbing potatoes, blood brothers of the culinary one, are happy-go-lucky plants with the same floral design as those of the kitchen garden, whose beauty often escapes the unobservant. Those that we can grow outdoors in this country, or parts of it, come within the nebulous category of floppers and scramblers, having no climbing mechanism; yet in their native South America they are inspired by an urgency to thrust their crowns high up into the branches of other trees and shrubs in order to reach the light.

This romping habit is the easiest and the most apt way in which to grow them, if a shrub host can be spared or if there is a low-roofed outhouse in the garden. There is a nice example of *Solanum crispum* clambering up a ceanothus at Sissinghurst.

Alternatively, they can be and usually are grown on a south wall, trellis or high fence, on which they must be tied and well displayed, instead of being allowed to degenerate into a tangled mop. They should be pruned by cutting the old flowered shoots fairly hard back to the old wood in late winter or early spring, but you need a sweet temper and much patience to do so. Any reasonable soil satisfies them but they want all the sun possible.

The two species of the climbing potato grown here are:

S. crispum. The best known and the hardier of the two, with pretty mauve flowers enhanced by conspicuous, golden stamens. It blooms with great freedom from midsummer until the autumn and behaves as an evergreen in the milder places. The variety 'Glasnevin' (or 'Autumnalis') is a great improvement on the species – more slenderly graceful in habit, more brilliant in colour, more generous in flowers and, to boot, hardier. It flourishes in many of the colder areas where it is given a south or south-west wall.

S. jasminoides § is one of our very finest climbers, shooting eagerly more than 20 feet high into a chosen tree or sprawling widely over a garage roof. It has glossy leaves, a slender carriage, and powder-blue flowers a little like the jasmine. Its white variety, *album*, is finer still, being massed with wide-open jasmine flowers, loosely and airily borne all the summer. Unfortunately, *S. jasminoides* is not nearly as hardy as *crispum* and must be confined to the warmer places.

Sophora §

Connoisseurs' trees of outstanding beauty but little hardiness. The graceful, wisteria-like foliage and the big clusters of yellow flowers, which seem never to be able to make up their minds whether to imitate the sweet-pea or the fuchsia, carry the hallmark of distinction, but do not disclose that they keep themselves within the pale of the most sheltered climates.

The species most widely grown is the celebrated kowhai of New Zealand, which is ***S. tetraptera.*** This has the faculty of losing its leaves if the weather gets cold, so has a fair chance in cooler areas, if protected from the north and east. However, it is scarcely a plant for small places, for it has a tree-like habit and, if it succeeds at all, will attain more than 30 feet and cannot well be expected to lie flat against a wall, although the young leading shoots can and should be tied in.

The kowhai has delightful ferny foliage and pendulous branches of golden flowers, loosely tubular, in May and June, followed by long and amusing seed pods. Even better than the parent species is its variety 'Grandiflora' which is larger both in flower and in leaf and a very fine plant for those who have room for it.

S. macrocarpa is a much smaller plant than *tetraptera* and so much more suitable to average houses and gardens. Though having rather larger leaflets, it is a very handsome plant decorated with crowded clusters of golden, loosely tubular flowers in May or earlier. It flowers at an early age.

Avoid *S. japonica*; it becomes a large tree and takes years to flower.

TRICUSPIDARIA. See *Crinodendron.*
VERONICA. See *Hebe.*

Winter's Bark

Drimys winteri

This beautiful evergreen is nearly hardy and needs wall protection only in colder counties. From glossy, olive-green foliage it produces compound umbels of flowers that have a daisy-like appearance, with ivory-white petals and yellow stamens. It likes a loamy soil and in the Gulf Stream counties will grow to 30 feet; inland against a wall, half that size, in time. Takes a few years to flower and when not in bloom the shrub much resembles a rhododendron. The whole plant has a sharply aromatic scent, especially in its bark and leaves.

Its very apt popular name is a conjunction of this quality of its bark and of John Winter, captain of one of Drake's ships, who brought it home. Its associations are also nicely summed up in its former and more euphonious botanical name, *Wintera aromatica.*

The variety *latifolia* has broader leaves and grows taller.

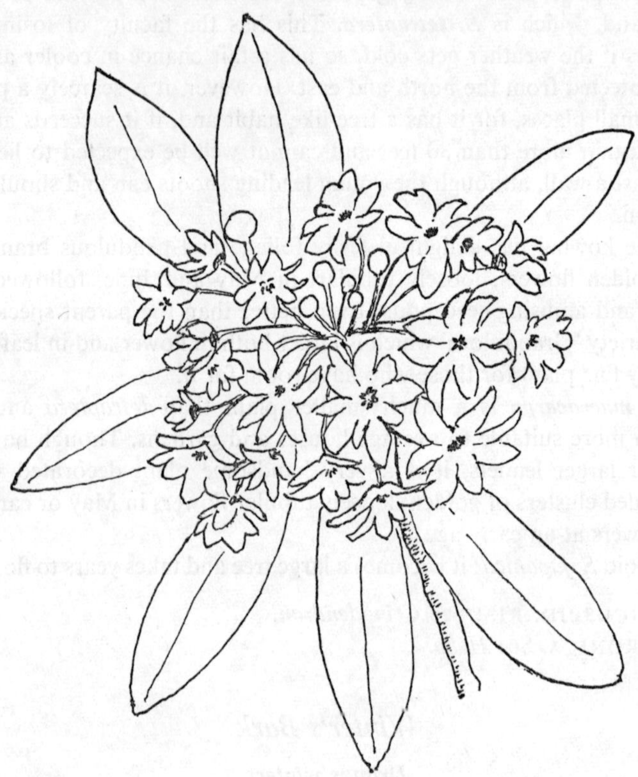

FIG. 27. Winter's Bark (*Drimys winteri*).

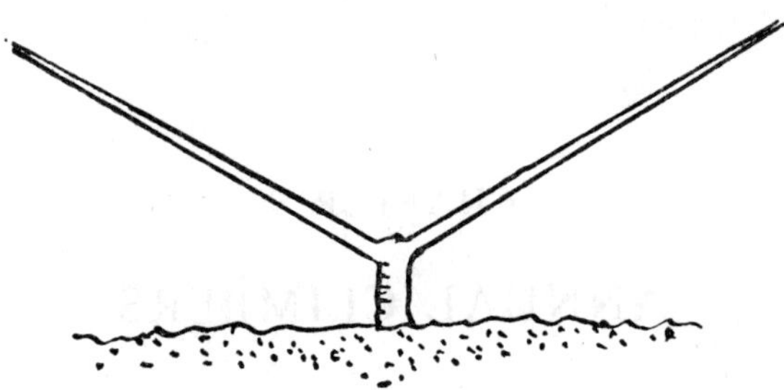

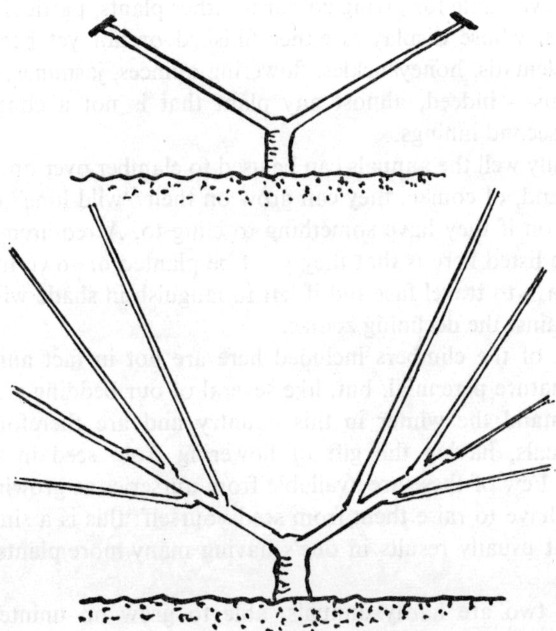

FIG. 28. Steps in the formal training of a cotoneaster fan.

(*a*) After a season to get established, two or more branches are led out and tied to canes fixed to the wall framework.

(*b*) Next winter the branches are cut back by at least one-third.

(*c*) In the following summer four new branches are trained out. These are cut back by at least one-third in the ensuing winter; and so on.

CHAPTER 9

ANNUAL CLIMBERS

To expect any plant to grow some 7 feet high from a seed in less than three months is asking a lot and yet there are several that, besides the climbing beans, will do so with gusto. All are easy to grow and they have a very useful part to play in the coloured drama of the garden. Apart from their own intrinsic attractions, they are valuable for giving colour to other plants, particularly other climbers, whose display is either finished or not yet begun. Thus roses, clematis, honeysuckles, flowering quinces, jasmines, celastrus, solanums – indeed, almost any plant that is not a clinger – can have a second innings.

Equally well the annuals can be used to clamber over open-ground plants and, of course, they can grow on their "wild lone" on arches and so on if they have something to cling to. A requirement of all that are listed here is that they must be planted or sown in full sun. They have to travel fast and if left to languish in shade will lose the race against the declining zodiac.

Most of the climbers included here are not in fact annuals and are in nature perennial, but, like several of our bedding plants, they rarely stand the winter in this country and are therefore treated as annuals, having the gift of flowering from seed in their first season. Few of these are available from nurseries as growing plants, so you have to raise them from seed yourself; this is a simple business but usually results in one's having many more plants than are needed.

Only two are hardy annuals, able to grow on uninterruptedly from seed sown straight into the ground in spring.

First and above all is the **sweet pea.** It has always seemed to me curious that sweet peas are so seldom allowed to grow in their natural carefree manner. We think of them only as stiffly trained cordon plants for the exhibitor or as clumps sown among miniature copses of hazel twigs. You can, however, grow them very decoratively at the foot of any plant on which they have a chance of clinging by their little tendrils. Their only essential demands otherwise are a good, rich soil, plenty of direct sun and the plucking off of seed pods as soon as the flowers wither.

If you want to do the job properly, you will raise the seedlings in the autumn, over-wintering them in a frame, or you will buy young plants from a nursery in the spring. All I do, however, is to pop the seed direct into the ground in March, an inch deep, usually among climbing roses, and nip out the growing tip of the seedling when about 4 inches high to make it branch. A few twigs may be necessary to give its tendrils a start. You are not likely by this means to win any sweet pea prizes at the flower-show, but you will have some pretty butterfly-flowers to greet you as you pass.

You may do the same sort of thing, if you have a mind to, with the common-or-garden climbing **"nasturtium"**, so-called; but in this case you sow where the soil is poor, for in rich soil you will get much leafage and little visible flower. Delay sowing until April. For my part, I never allow *Tropaeolum majus*, climbing or otherwise, in my garden, for it is a magnet to all the black fly in the county.

The popular yellow **canary creeper,** which is *Tropaeolum peregrinum*, is rather more tender and should be treated as a half-hardy. It is a pretty little climber with leaves deeply cleft into lobes and with yellow flowers serrated in the upper petals and shaggily fringed in the lower ones and looking altogether like a tiny bird in flight. Here again poor soil is best. Its alternative name is *T. canariensis*.

All those that now follow are also treated as half-hardy annuals. They include some very attractive things that are most surprisingly neglected in the average garden. They cannot be planted out in the open ground until the last week of May in the south or the first week of June in the north. Following the same drill as for antirrhinums, asters, etc., the seed is therefore sown in the usual shallow boxes or in pots in March, brought on in a slightly heated greenhouse or frame (or on the inside window-sill of the kitchen), pricked out into other boxes or pots after the first true leaves have fully expanded and hardened off in early May. If they progress fast when pricked out into a second box, they must be potted, so one may as well pot them at the first move.

The following is the choice before us.

Cobaea scandens is a slender, fast-growing plant, clinging by corkscrew tendrils and breaking out into carillons of delightful flowers very like Canterbury bells with very prominent stamens and pistil and a large, expanding, saucer-like calyx. The flowers start white, become green, develop a mauve blush and finally turn deep purple. The first flowers usually arrange themselves obligingly at or near eye level, so that one can peer into their queerly beautiful caverns. They are thus particularly good plants for climbing on climbers on a pergola or trellis and are great fun rushing up a hedge.

Be sure not to be late in sowing and raising the cobaea, otherwise only a few of its flowers will open before the cold weather. The seed seems to germinate more freely if sown on edge. It will grow quite 15 feet high in a summer and, in very genial climates (or in greenhouses), a good deal higher. Technically, the cobaea is a perennial, but can be treated as such only in a greenhouse.

Eccremocarpus scaber is the devil of a name for a pretty little climber that is as easy as pie to grow. Botanically, this also is a perennial and indeed behaves as such in a mild winter. Having delicate, rather anemone-like foliage, it shoots up as rapidly as the cobaea, but not as far, and is festooned, rather sparsely, with clusters of small, orange, tubular flowers. I grow them usually on a fastigiate hawthorn and on climbing roses.

Morning Glory is a name popularly applied to several closely related plants, but the best of the lot is one that in my youth we used to call simply a convolvulus of sorts. Now, if you want to be sure of getting the right thing, you take a deep breath and demand *Ipomoea rubro-caerulea* 'Praecox'. Or you may ask for the variety 'Heavenly Blue'.

These, in a good summer and in the mornings only, will give those marvellous bugles or funnels of a vivid, luminous, incandescent blue that makes one "stand and stare". Each flower lasts no time at all, but is quickly replaced from the fascinating mechanism of the slender, spirally coiled buds. The plant is a twiner, and ascends its host in such the same, neat, exact and methodical way as our native bindweed or bellbind. Rather poor and stony soils are better than lush ones, which cause excessive leaf growth and few flowers.

As in the cobaea, you must get the ipomoea under way quickly also. If you buy your seed from a shop, you may find no other

Annual climbers. *Above: Eccremocarpus scaber*

Below: 'Morning Glory', *Ipomoea caerulea*

Cobaea scandens

The hop, *Humulus lupulus*

Hoya carnosa

name on the packet but 'Morning Glory', or you may find various others names, but all morning glories are good of their kind. There are also varieties in other colours than blue, including the lavender 'Wedding Bells', the red 'Scarlet O'Hara' and the pink-and-gold 'Hearts and Honey'. To hasten germination, make a little nick in the seed with a file. Sow in peat pots to avoid root disturbance when planting out. They are good hedge-climbers.

"Black-eyed Susan" is a name given to two or three plants (which is the danger of all vernacular names) but the one for us here is the jolly, half-hardy stem-twiner ***Thunbergia alata.*** As climbers go, it is a shorty, not often reaching much more than 4 feet. The flower is tubular, expanding widely to a bell-like mouth. There are several colour varieties – yellow, white, cream and, best of all, orange; most have the deep, dark purple throat that provides the clue to its popular names. Seedsmen have their own pet names for the various colour forms and you may, if you wish, buy a packet of mixed colours. A fairly high temperature, in the region of 65° F. is needed for germination of the seed.

In the United States this thunbergia is also known as the 'Clock vine'.

The **maurandya** is not often seen outside greenhouses, but is perfectly well adapted to the outdoors by the usual half-hardy annual treatment, provided a temperature of about 60° can be given for germinating the seed. The climbing species, which hang on by twisting their long leaf stalks round their hosts, are quite exciting plants to have about the garden. The usual one is *M. barclaiana*, which gives us funnel-shaped flowers that may be 3 inches long and of diverse colours – purple, rose or white; they are soon over but are freely produced. Both the genus and the species are frequently mis-spelt.

Very good also is *M. erubescens*, with large, rosy blooms freely borne all summer, but the seed is not easy to get. Other good ones are *M. lophospermum*, with large, rosy-purple flowers, and *M. scandens*, with smaller flowers in blended colours.

Gourds. Blood brothers of our vegetable marrow, but quite uneatable, the ornamental gourds are great fun to grow and are amusing decorations for bowls and dishes in the house throughout the winter. Fantasy could scarcely be more freely expressed than in their many shapes and colours. Here you will find fruits masquerading as oranges, as pears, as a child's green ball, as football jerseys in green and yellow and, most fascinating of all, as bright red turbans such as Turks used to wear before they became drably Westernized.

You can buy a packet of mixed seeds which will give you a few of these styles, but it is much more satisfactory, I think, to buy the varieties separately; then you can be sure of the turbans, which are the most fun. Sow the seeds singly, straight into small pots and pot-on as necessary.

You can employ these gourds decoratively in various ways but best of all, I think, over an arch or along a trellis or fence; not, I suggest, on a house-wall. You must give them all the sun you can, tie them up as they grow (for they are not genuine climbers) and prevent the fruits from lying on the ground, where they will get pulpy and be attacked by slugs.

Hops. The hop is an express-speed climber and is one of the best plants for providing a quick screen of leafage where one may be wanted or for mantling an arch. Its finely designed leaves are also very decorative, especially in the variegated Japanese species, which is *Humulus japonicus* 'Variegatus'. For quick results, raise it in the manner of a half-hardy annual, like all the others we have been discussing.

Quamoclit. The quamoclits are pretty little stem-twiners for use when one is in search of something new. They are true annuals, rushing up to 7 feet by July and flowering till the autumn, when the plants die.

The flowers are small, pouchy tubes with expanded mouths and are accompanied by dark green, lacy foliage. I doubt whether it is much use trying to grow them outdoors except in the warmer counties, but elsewhere they are easy enough in slightly heated greenhouses.

Give them the usual treatment for half-hardy annuals, then put them out in full sun and give them a lot of water throughout the summer.

The two species grown here are:

Q. lobata, whose flowers begin crimson, wane to orange and then to yellow.

Q. pennata, scarlet.

Various synonyms of the quamoclit are bandied about as a result of botanical fervour. *Mina* is the most usual, as most seedsmen funk "quamoclit".

Although not an annual, the climbing **monkshood** (*Aconitum* *volubile*) is most conveniently included in this chapter. It is a hardy herbaceous perennial, climbing to some 12 feet by slender, twining stems and bearing small clusters of the usual helmet-shaped flowers in violet. Easy enough from seed, it flowers from August onwards. Not distinguished when alone, but a good "climber on climber".

CHAPTER 10

GREENHOUSE CLIMBERS

No doubt the reader who does not live in the envied Gulf Stream counties will have been infuriated by the repeated examples in previous chapters of plants that are so tantalizingly out of his grasp. He may take heart, however, if he has a bit of glass sufficiently warmed to take off the rough edge of the cold – a formal greenhouse, a glazed porch, loggia or veranda or an old Victorian conservatory. A great many of the slightly tender plants will thrive in such places. I do not imagine that climbing plants will often be grown in them for their own sakes alone, but they have the great virtue of turning what may otherwise look like a mere glass workshop into a prettily furnished floral drawing-room.

In this chapter I shall limit myself to those plants that are satisfied by "cool" conditions in which a minimum temperature of 40° F can be maintained "when icicles hang by the wall" and "milk come frozen home in pail". To attempt to deal also with the flowers of the "warm" house – (minimum temperature 55°) and the "hot" house (70°) would extend the scope too far and would carry me into realms of which my knowledge is limited. Those who are fortunate enough to be able to maintain warm and hot houses may luxuriate in the ambrosial sweetness of the stephanotis and the gardenia, may surround themselves with the imperial purple of the tibouchinas or in imagination listen to the chimes of the allamanda's golden bells; but we, in our cool houses, have yet some splendours of our own and some may be grown even in a greenhouse with no heat at all.

I have to take it for granted that the reader has already some knowledge of greenhouse management and understands the small skills of hygiene, ventilation, watering and the maintenance of a "buoyant atmosphere".[1] But there are a few points touching climbers in particular that ought to be registered.

In the first place, it will be obvious that only a few climbers are suited to very small houses – such as eccremocarpus, thunbergia and billardiera. What is less obvious is that the modern metal house does not easily lend itself to climbers, because of the difficulty of fixing nails, wires and other gadgets to provide the hosts that are of course needed just as much as outdoors. The Dutch-light type of house, with glass right down to the ground, is also not very good, for it needs an awful lot of heating, is subject to violent fluctuations of temperature and in summer will cause the leaves of those that do not like too fierce a glare to be scorched.

Thus, for our purposes, the old-fashioned style of house with a wooden framework resting on low walls of brick, concrete or timber, is the best and the larger the better. Here the means of climbing are easily provided by straining wires across the rafters, every foot or so. The wooden lean-to greenhouses, especially the three-quarter span type, are also excellent, for climbers can be beautifully and simply displayed along the brick or stone wall against which the glasswork is built, using straining wires or trellis as a host.

A few plants, particularly the lapageria, will need sun-blinds at the height of the summer. Several types are on the market and I think that the best for us is the exterior type made of cedarwood lathes, which give the effect of dappled sunlight.[2] In general, climbers will be better planted in a border in the greenhouse, but there are plenty that are quite happy in tubs or large pots. In the latter case, however, they should be potted on by degrees – from small pots to larger ones as each becomes filled with roots until they are ready for their final receptacles.

The soil in the border, for general purposes, had best be a mixture of two parts rich, fibrous, turf loam, one part peat and one part sharp sand; and the drainage must be above suspicion. For pots, John Innes Potting Compost No. 2 is usually suitable.

Although I have assumed some general knowledge on the reader's part, there are two cultural directives which it is important to follow

[1] *The Small Greenhouse*, by H. Witham Fogg, published by Pan Books, is a good primer on the subject. *Electricity in Your Garden*, published by the Electrical Development Association, Savoy Hill, London, is a valuable guide to electrical greenhouse installations and management.

[2] Robert Hall and Co., Tunbridge Wells, are good providers of sun-blinds.

for nearly all plants in this chapter. They concern watering and ventilation and may be set down in short terms thus:

Water all borders, tubs and pots liberally in spring and summer, ease off in winter and leave the soil on the dry side in winter.

Ventilate the house freely at all seasons consistent with keeping out fog and frost.

Climbers are a very permanent feature of the greenhouse and the gardener must decide for himself which will consort best with any other plants that he wants to grow. There is no room for communism in the greenhouse. Not all its occupants will accept the same conditions. In heat, light, water and soil many will expect their special privileges. Except when planted against a wall of a lean-to, all but the very shortest climbers and the least dense in foliage will keep out a lot of light. That condition will, indeed, be very acceptable by such plants as begonias, gloxinias and streptocarpus, but will not be tolerated by carnations, pelargoniums, the lordly hippeastrums nor the proletarian tomato.

The list that follows includes virtually all the climbers that require and that can be successfully grown in cool conditions. Several are easy. The majority are plants that have appeared in previous chapters and that can be grown under glass in districts too cold for their outdoor culture. Some that I would specially commend are the lapageria, the plumbago, the tender jasmines, the mandevilla and *Solanum jasminoides*. Of course, many of the "Gulf Stream" wall shrubs may also be grown under glass where there is room for them.

Aristolochia

See Chapter 7. Not really worth greenhouse space, especially as it expects a rich soil, but *A. macrophylla* may be useful in such places as porches or loggias for its foliage and for the fact that it is very nearly hardy and wants a fire only in extra fierce winters. Ventilate freely.

Bignonia

As we have noted in Chapter 7, the botanists have almost annihilated the once flourishing bignonia tribe. Among those they have banished is the handsome *B. venusta*, but I am including it here as it is still the most widely used name. A tendril climber, it is one of the "trumpet vines", close cousin to the campsis we have noticed in Chapter 6, and produces trumpets of brilliant orange in pendulous clusters. A winter minimum temperature of 40° will keep it in sufficiently good health, but an extra 10° will make all the difference and prolong its flowering season for several weeks.

Water freely in summer, keeping a moist atmosphere, but very little in winter. Best planted in the border with a rich soil and plenty of sun. In winter prune the shoots back to about one-third. The orthodox name now is *Pyrostegia venusta*.

See also *Bignonia capreolata* (Chapter 7), which is easy enough in a large, cool greenhouse.

Billardiera

See Chapter 7. Though not in the front row of the chorus, *B. longiflora* is a useful twiner because it is of modest growth, evergreen and slender-stemmed. It suits a small porch very well and is quite happy in a pot filled with John Innes No. 2 Potting Compost.

Another species that can be grown under the protection of glass is *B. scandens*, with cream flowers from June to September, but not so good as its brother.

Cobaea

See Chapter 9. Grown under glass, *C. scandens* develops into quite a considerable size, racing well up into the rafters of a fairly big house, but it can be kept in check and its performance improved by pruning it fairly hard in February. It will, of course, behave as the perennial that it is. It needs no heat until the approach of hard weather, then just enough to keep out the frost is all that is needed.

Give plenty of air and water in spring and summer.

Eccremocarpus

See Chapter 9. The pretty little *E. scaber* is an easy one to grow in a small greenhouse or a porch and will behave as a perennial in even an unheated one unless a very severe winter occurs. It will be content in a medium sized pot.

Hoya

One of the most popular and prettiest of all climbing plants for the slightly heated greenhouse is *H. carnosa.* It is a very slim and flexible twiner, which bursts out into tightly packed clusters of small, fleshy, pallid pink flowers that look as though they have been carved from wax. You would think from its general appearance that it was a very tender, shy creature, needing much cosseting, for its shoots look very frail and its maiden's-blush flowers look anything but rugged. It will, in fact, appreciate a winter minimum of 45°, but I have known it to cling to life even when the thermometer was nearly down to freezing.

One of the charms of this hoya is that it submits with willingness and grace to being displayed in all sorts of manners. With the aid of a few canes you can bend it round in a circle, like a cart wheel. You can corkscrew it round a pillar. You can string it along the rafters. Moreover, if planted close against the wall of a lean-to greenhouse, it may well surprise you by turning from a twiner into a clinger, putting out little holdfasts or "aerial roots" like an ivy.

The hoya has a remarkably long season of bloom, but is in full beauty in July and August. It likes to be planted in the border, but will do very well indeed in a large pot or small tub, provided it is re-potted not less often than once every three years, an operation that is done in March.

Several other hoyas can be grown in warm houses; but *H. globulosa,* which is deep cream, and possibly one or two more, can be grown in the same conditions of *carnosa,* if you can get them.

IPOMOEA. See Morning Glory.

Jasmine

See Chapter 8. The primrose jasmine and the honey-scented *J. polyanthum* are among the most cherished plants for greenhouses not too small to accommodate them.

Another candidate is *J. grandiflorum*, which flowers from June to September. Its flowers resemble those of the summer jasmine, but it is not so attractive a plant as the others, being in nature a straggling shrub.

All these jasmines will be satisfied with tubs or large pots if there is not room to spare in the border. Plant them in March and water them as prescribed in the opening section of this chapter.

Other species, such as the Arabian jasmine (*J. sambac*) need warmer houses.

Lapageria

See Chapter 7. Without doubt, *Lapageria rosea* is the queen of cool greenhouse climbers. Plant it in March in the border or in a large tub. Water it copiously all the spring and summer. In the summer spray it daily to create a slightly humid atmosphere and keep the blinds pulled down except on dull days. Stream the plant along the rafters a trifle above eye level, so that its wonderful carillons of ruby bells can be seen in their full beauty.

Mandevilla

See Chapter 7. The jasmine-like beauty and the honeyed scent of *M. suaveolens* and the very similar *tweediana* put them among the most desired plants in the cool greenhouse. They do not take kindly to pots, however, so should be planted on the border, though no doubt a large tub would prove successful. Where a glazed porch, loggia or veranda forms part of the dwelling house, I can imagine the mandevilla as a charming adornment and in such a case a tub would be the only choice.

Maurandya

See Chapter 9. *M. barclaiana* and its brother species are charming decorations in very small or large houses. They are quite happy in pots and some of the shoots can be allowed to hang down instead of being led upwards. Or they can be treated altogether as trailers and planted in a hanging basket. In the greenhouse they become perennial and should be cut back hard in February.

MINA. See *Quamoclit* in Chapter 9 and below.

Morning Glory

See Chapter 9. The diverse varieties of *Ipomoea rubro-caerulea* become perennial in a greenhouse where a winter temperature of 50° is maintained, but there is a good chance in the milder counties of their doing so at lower temperatures also. They are agreeable to tubs and 8-inch pots, but prefer the border.

The magnificent "blue dawn flower", which used to be *I. learii*, but is now *Pharbitis learii*, seen in opulent splendour in the French Riviera, needs warmer conditions than those allowed for in this chapter.

Plumbago

One of the easiest as well as one of the most beautiful of climbers for a cool house is *P. capensis*. It is embellished with clusters of flowers that resemble the phlox in Cambridge blue – a colour much to be desired in the greenhouse. It is very nearly a hardy plant, especially if against the wall of a lean-to, and I grew it for years in a small greenhouse that had no more heating than an oil lamp kept in reserve for the very coldest weather. It is *the* beginner's climber, and, however familiar one may become over the years with more difficult plants, the Cape plumbago never loses its freshness and charm.

It will grow fairly big – certainly 12 feet high or long and I dare say more – and spread widely. The wall of a lean-to house is therefore the place to display its beauty best, though there is, of course, no reason why it should not be trained up between the rafters. Plant it in March in a border if you can, alternatively in a fair-sized tub or outsize pot. Ventilate freely and spray the foliage daily in spells of hot weather.

The Cape plumbago flowers throughout most of the summer on shoots that have developed in the current season and these shoots should be cut back hard when flowering finishes. This will ensure an even display of bloom and restrain excessive top growth. Let the soil in the border, tub or pot go fairly dry in winter, in order to give the plant a period of rest.

There is also a white form of this plumbago, but the blue is the thing.

Quamoclit

See Chapter 9. For greenhouse use move the seedlings on to 6-inch pots as soon as they are ready and keep them well watered.

Roses

Two climbing roses are particularly associated with cool (or even cold) greenhouses, as they are supposedly on the danger line of hardiness. These are the fine old 'Maréchal Niel', a beautiful rose of soft gold, richly scented, and the other is the white 'Climbing Niphetos'. In a very cold part of the Mendips we grew 'Maréchal Niel' in a 14-foot lean-to, entirely unheated because of the war; covering the whole of its stone wall, it never failed to bloom and filled the whole place with its sweet essence. The culture is exactly the same as for roses outdoors, except that you must keep a look-out for the special pests of the greenhouse. Ventilate very freely at all seasons consistent with keeping out frost and fog.

Solanum

See Chapter 7. *S. jasminoides* is one of the most beautiful and most richly scented of all climbers for a greenhouse, but it expects to be given plenty of room. Its white, jasmine-like flowers bloom nearly all the summer, embalming the air with their fragrance. It will take to a tub or a large pot if space in the border cannot be spared and it is so nearly hardy that it needs only just enough heat to keep out the frost.

If it threatens to outgrow its territory, this solanum will suffer being cut back in winter and, as the plant ages, worn-out stems can be eliminated. Water liberally in spring and summer.

Tecomaria

Another outcast from the tecoma tribe, the "Cape honeysuckle" (*T. capensis*) is a strong climber with agreeable, pinnate foliage and showy trusses of brilliant orange-scarlet flowers in the form of curved tubes with widely flared mouths. Very gay and lively, the florets have a distinct resemblance to those of the honeysuckle and break into bloom in late summer. The smooth stems will reach to 14 feet, yet the roots will be content in a large pot.

Thunbergia alata

We have met "Black-eyed Susan" in the last chapter. It is very easy and suitable for a greenhouse or porch, content with a 5-inch pot and asking for only the minimum degree of warmth, except for germination of its seed. Let it have plenty of sun and fresh air. It will behave as a perennial or you can sow seed afresh each spring.

There are several other thunbergias, annual and perennial, including the very large *grandiflora* and *gregorii (gibsonii)*.

Trachelospermum

See Chapter 7. *T. jasminoides* is one of the most attractive and sweetest greenhouse climbers in districts that are too cold for its outdoor culture, but it will need a fairly big one. Its evergreen, glossy nature is an added attraction. The slender shoots can be fanned out along the wall of a lean-to house or can be led up and along the rafters in any house, where, however, they will cast a lot of shade. It needs only the minimum of winter warmth.

APPENDIX

By no means all the plants mentioned in this book will be obtainable at the average nursery, but all will be found at one or another of the following:

Bodnant Garden, Tal y Cafn, Colwyn Bay, North Wales. (Many rare plants.)

Slieve Donard Nursery Co., Newcastle, County Down, Northern Ireland. (Many "Gulf Stream" plants.)

Hillier & Sons, Winchester. (The most complete list.)

George Jackman & Sons, Woking.

R. C. Notcutt Ltd., Woodbridge, Suffolk.

John Scott & Co, The Royal Nurseries, Merriott, Somerset.

Sunningdale Nurseries, Windlesham, Surrey.

John Waterer, Sons and Crisp, Bagshot, Surrey.

For roses there are many specialists, but most varieties can be obtained from the last six nurserymen.

Clematis specialists include:

Christopher Lloyd, Great Dixter, Northiam, Sussex.

Pennell & Sons, Lincoln.

Fisk's Nursery, Westleton, Saxmundham, Suffolk.

George Jackman & Sons, Woking.

INDEX

INDEX

The figures in **bold** type indicate the main passages dealing with cultivation and the selection of varieties, as distinct from other references.

ADDENDUM

Forsythia - Lynwood species

Skimmia japonica

Nobelle

In Kew ?

Stachyuraceae

6-8 ft

Ginkgo

Royal gold

Rhododendron -

Ericaceae racemosum

- more leafy praecox

than praecox

? Desfontainea spinosa

? Crinodendron hookerianum

? Pileostegia

Russian vine (polygonum baldschuanicum)